rather*newyorkcity*

*researched, written and photographed by julia oh, kaie wellman, anna h. blessing, jan faust dane,
camas davis and jon hart*

toc

neighborhoods

EAT

2nd avenue deli
abraço • barbarini
beer table
birdbath bakery
bklyn larder • blaue gans
brooklyn flea • buvette
café sabarsky
classic coffee shop
di fara pizza • dirt candy
double crown • dough
dovetail • dutch kills
eat greenpoint
flushing, queens
dumpling crawl
fort defiance • gottino
henry public • home/made
hung ry • i sodi
james • joseph leonard
king of falafel & shawarma
lexington candy shop
lucali • manducatis
mast brothers chocolate
mayahuel
mei li wah bakery
mile end • mimi's hummus
miss mamie's
spoonbread too
no.7 • northern spy food co.
num pang • peaches
philoxenia • porchetta
prime meats • roberta's
roman's • saltie
saraghina • sunrise mart
takashi • the beagle
the breslin
the farm on adderley
the fat radish
the hungarian pastry shop
the redhead • the smile
the ten bells • txikito
vanessa's dumpling house
van leeuwen
artisan ice cream
vinegar hill house
xi'an famous foods
zibetto

SHOP

acorn • adeline adeline
assembly new york
b-4 it was cool
brook farm general store
change of season • c'h'c'm
clic bookstore & gallery
complete traveller
antiquarian bookstore
creatures of comfort
dear : rivington+
erie basin • eva gentry
extra • fenton fallon
gesamtkunstwerk
greenwich letterpress
haus interior • hollander & lexer
holler & squall
hyman hendler & sons
joanne hendricks, cookbooks...
john derian company
johnson trading gallery
jumelle • kill devil hill
kiosk • leffot
loren • maryam nassir zadeh
matta
meg cohen design shop
min new york • moscot
nili lotan • no. 6 store
no. 8b
obscura antiques and oddities
occulter • ochre store
palmer trading company
partners & spade
pasanella and son vintners
philip williams posters
pomme • reed space
saipua • saturdays surf nyc
smith + butler • stock vintage
store 518 • sweet william
swing: a concept shop
szeki • the banquet
the crangi family project
victor osborne • voos
wendy nichol
zero + maria cornejo

notes about nyc

rather *new york city* EDITORS >

Julia Oh was raised in a toy store and blessed with 11 stomachs, Julia Oh writes and produces film in NYC

Kaie Wellman is the creator of the *eat.shop guides* and *rather*. Though a lover of pretty objects and fine food, Kaie loves puffy down vests and donuts.

Anna H. Blessing has authored scads of *eat.shop* books and also contributes to Design*Sponge and other publications with the BBB Craft Sisters.

Jan Faust Dane is one of the original *eat. shop* editors and is also a professional food forager.

Camas Davis is a writer and editor, but likes to get her hands dirty, so now she's also a butcher.

Jon Hart is a jack-of-all-trades, currently trying to master relaxation. His other accomplishments include eating and drinking.and a lover of all things weird and wonderful.

KW: If there was a reality show called *Survivor: Big City*, I have no doubt that New York City would be victorious. Since its founding as New Amsterdam in 1624 and forty years later becoming New York City, the big island (Manhattan) and its four sibling boroughs (Bronx, Queens, Brooklyn, and Staten Island) have withstood some tough times—from the battles of the American Revolution to being on the verge of bankruptcy in the '70s to 9/11 and now the Great Recession. But this tenacious city has battled back like Omarosa, righteously keeping its mantle as the most exciting, vibrant city this side of Mars.

The small local eating and shopping establishments of this city have been hit hard. A number of great places that were doing great before 2008 have closed their doors.So we hit the streets, looking for good news. After criscrossing the city from north to south, east to west, we chose 125 amazing small, locally owned businesses that were flourishing.

I can't say enough about these businesses. Some have been around for almost a hundred years, some have been open two months. Some are high-end, some won't cost you more than an Alexander Hamilton to enjoy. While many are embracing an early 1900s aesthetic, others are looking towards the future. What they all have in common is that they embrace the "keep on, keepin' on" spirit, and are doing it with aplomb.

Though this book is all about the local eating and shopping experience, we can offer up some suggestions for other activities around the city. Here you go:

1 > On the Water: NYC and Brooklyn are basically islands. Paddle around Brooklyn in a rented kayak or canoe launched from Red Hook piers; or adventure straight through Brooklyn on the Gowanus Canal.

2 > The High Line: The most highly anticipated "park" to open in NYC since Central Park opened in 1859. Running from Gansevoort Street in the Meatpacking District up through Chelsea, this is a great place to take a breather and the view across the Hudson.

3 > Red Hook Ball Fields: Okay, this involves eating. But the fields were closing for the season when we were in production on this book. From mid-April through October this is the place to come on the weekends for great Latino food.

it's all about...

exploring locally

*discovering a sense of place
behind the veneer of a city*

*experiencing what gives
a city its soul through its
local flavor*

rather EVOLUTION

If you are thinking this book looks suspiciously like an *eatshop guide*, you're on to something. As of October 2011, the *eatshop guide* evolved into **rather** to give readers a more vibrant experience when it comes to local eating and shopping. It's all about what you'd **rather** be doing with your time when you explore a city—eat at a chain restaurant or an intimate little trattoria devouring dishes the chef created from farm fresh ingredients? You get the idea.

USING **rather**

All of the businesses featured in this book are first and foremost locally owned, and they are chosen to be featured because they are authentic and uniquely conceived. And since this isn't an advertorial guide, there's no money exchanging hands • Make sure to double check the hours of the business before you go, as many places change their hours seasonally • The pictures and descriptions for each business are meant to give a feel for a place, but please know those items may no longer be available • Our maps are stylized, meaning they don't show every street • Small local businesses have always had to work that much harder to keep their heads above water, and not all the businesses featured will stay open. Please go to **rather** website for updates • **rather** editors research, shoot and write everything you see in this book • Only natural light is used to shoot and there's no styling or propping.

restaurants >
$ = inexpensive $$ = medium $$$ = expensive

Go to **rather.com** to learn more

where to lay your weary head

for more hotel choices, visit >

NewYorkHotel.net

PART OF THE TRAVELSHARK
TRAVEL NETWORK

---

the james hotel
27 grand street (soho / tribeca)
212.465.2000 / jameshotels.com
standard double from $290
restaurant: david burke kitchen bar: jimmy
notes: environmentally thoughtful hotel with
stunning views of downtown

the ace hotel
20 west 29th street (murray hill)
212.679.2222 / acehotel.com
standard double from $150
restaurant: the breslin
notes: west coast utilitarian chic comes east

hotel americano
518 west 27th street (chelsea)
212.216.0000 / hotel-americano.com
standard double from $255
restaurant: the americano
notes: first stateside hotel from uber-cool
mexican hotel group

the nolitan
30 kenmare street (nolita)
212.925.2555 / nolitanhotel.com
standard double from $240
restaurant: ellabess
notes: private balconies overlooking downtown,
free skateboard rentals

the shoreham
33 west 55th street (midtown)
212.247.6700 / shorehamhotel.com
standard double from $249
bar: shorham bar
notes: central location and pillow top mattresses

the nu hotel
85 smith street (park slope)
718.852-8585 / nuhotelbrooklyn.com
standard double from $200
notes: one of the only boutique hotels in
brooklyn

more eating gems

these businesses appeared in previous editions of eat.shop nyc and eat.shop brooklyn

EAT

a bistro
al di là
alma
angel's share
barney greengrass
bohemian hall beer garden
bierkraft
brown café
candle 79
casellula
cha an
chip shop
choice market
danal
d'amico foods
diner
dressler
dumont
egg
eisenberg's
feet sau
flor de mayo
frankie's 457 sputino
franny's
freemans
grandaisy bakery
habana outpost
ici
il laboratorio del gelato
jackson diner
joe & pat's
keens steakhouse
kefi
kyotofu
la luncheonette
locanda vini e olii
marlow & sons
mary's fish camp
mas (farmhouse)
moto
myers of keswick
odessa
one girl cookies
otafuku
pasita

pies n thighs
pop burger
poseidon greek bakery
prune
roasting plant coffee co.
roomali
rosenthal wine merchant
sahadi's
sal's pizzeria
saxelby cheesemongers
sfoglia
shanghai cafe
staubitz market
steve's authentic
key lime pie
taim falafel & smoothie bar
the good fork
the greene grape
the little owl
the spotted pig
tia pol
tony & tiny's pizza

more shopping gems

*these businesses appeared in
previous editions of eat.shop nyc
and eat.shop brooklyn*

SHOP

a detacher
allan & suzi
alpana bawa
amarcord
annelore
bblessing
bird
bonnie slotnick cookbooks
brooklyn general barber
bu and the duck
castor & pollux
cb i hate perfume
city joinery
cog & pearl
cozbi
d / l cerney
darr
de vera
e. vogel
elizabeth street gallery
freemans sporting club
golden calf
grdn
global table
halcyon the shop
hats. by bunn.
in god we trust
j. leon lascof & son
jutta neumann
kid o
layla
lord willy's
loveday 31
mantiques modern
matter
maxilla and mandible
mick margo

mini jake
mini mini market
moon river chattel
oak
odin (pas de deux)
purl / purl patchwork
roberta freymann
roberta roller rabbit
secondhand rose
the future perfect
the paris apartment
tinsel trading company
wonk
woodley & bunny
yoya / yoyamart

brooklyn

ditmas park, midwood

eat

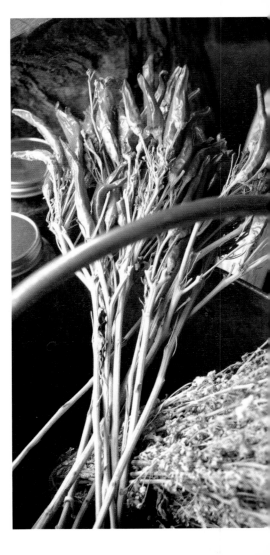

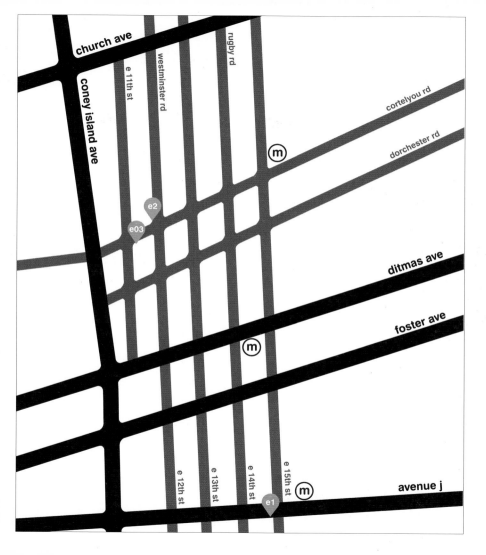

di fara pizza

legendary brooklyn pizza

1424 Avenue J
Corner of 15th (Midwood) *map E01*
Q: Avenue J
718.258.1367
www.difara.com

twitter @difara
wed - sun noon - 4:30p, 6 - 9p
lunch. dinner
$-$$ cash only. first come, first served

Yes, Please: *coca cola, ginger ale; pizza: plain pie, square pie, artichoke pie, special pie; cheese & prosciutto calzone*

CD: When Domenico DeMarco pulls a pizza from the ancient oven at Di Fara, he often uses his bare hands to do so. His gnarled and floured digits are those of a true master—one who's been stretching dough, grating mozzarella and snipping fresh basil since 1964. If there's any music playing here it's classical, but often it's silent, and everyone standing in line whispers as if at church, waiting for the sermon to begin. Indeed, we are all here to worship at **Di Fara**'s altar. And when we finally take that first bite of salty, cheesy, tangy, crunchy perfection, a communal murmur can be heard: yes, there is a God after all.

mimi's hummus

charming middle-eastern spot

1209 Cortelyou Road
Between Westminster and Argyle
(Ditmas Park) *map E02*
Q: Cortelyou Road
718.284.4444
www.mimishummus.com

mon - fri noon - 10:30p
sat - sun 11a - 10:30p
lunch. dinner
$-$$ first come, first served

Yes, Please: *fresh mint & sage tea, turkish coffee, masabache hummus, fava bean hummus, shakshuka eggs, stuffed grape leaves, eggplant caviar, housemade cookies*

AB: Time is at a premium in this city, where the term "bustling with energy" is a laughable understatement. So who has the time to leave his or her own sphere to eat? This was the question on my mind when I trekked to Ditmas Park to eat at **Mimi's Hummus**. Would anybody in their right (i.e., harried) mind make this trip for hummus? The answer is yes. I would happily have flown halfway around the world to Israel to eat this food. So slow down for a moment and remind yourself that a quick trip on the Q train is well worth it for a little bit of hummus heaven.

the farm on adderley

farm-fresh, seasonal ingredients

1108 Cortelyou Road
Between 11th and 12th
(Ditmas Park) *map E03*
Q: Cortelyou Road
718.287.3101
www.thefarmonadderley.com

twitter @farmonadderley
see website for hours
breakfast. lunch. dinner. brunch
$$ reservations accepted for parties of
five or more

Yes. Please: *ommegang abbey, grilled eggplant toast, hen of the wood mushroom tempura, pan-roasted pollack, short rib ravioli, french fries with curry mayo*

AB: Over the last couple of years, the locavore movement has taken hold of New York City, especially in Brooklyn, where urban farmers are digging up their tiny backyards (if they are lucky enough to have one) to grow vegetables and raise chickens. Though this sounds idyllic, let's be frank—there are not a lot of people living in the city who have the resources to do this. So what to do if you're hankering to eat farm-fresh food? Easy. Just amble over to **The Farm on Adderley.** Everything here is hand-chosen from local purveyors, and the food is simple, homey and downright delicious. Yee-haw.

brooklyn

redhook

eat

shop

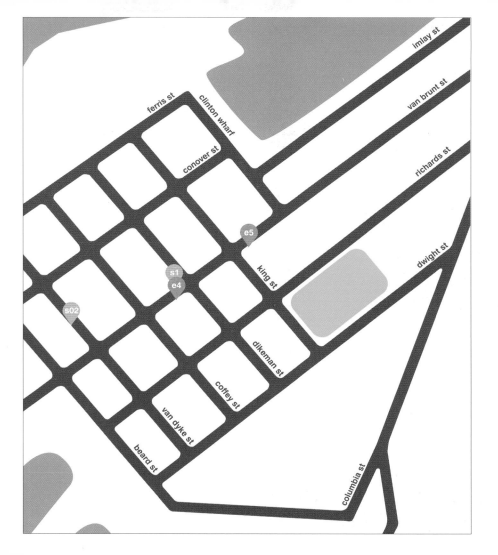

erie basin

*eclectic antiques, furniture, jewelry
sand folk art*

**388 Van Brunt Street
Between Dikeman and Coffey
(Red Hook)** *map S01*
**Bus: 61/77
718.554.6147
www.eriebasin.com**

twitter @eriebasin
wed noon - 6p thu - sat noon - 7p
sun - tue by appointment only
online shopping

Yes, Please: *conroy+wilcox rose cut black diamond ring,
giant victorian hair comb, empire mahogany recamier,
early 1800s portait of mary on ivory, lee hale thorn studs*

CD: I wish I had bought that white porcelain wing I saw at Erie Basin. I'd made the stupid assumption that there were other stores like it that would have other wings like that, but I haven't found anything remotely similar since. Why? Because **Erie Basin** is like no other store. Many of the pieces here are one-of-a-kind, whether antique or contemporary. Owner Russell Whitmore picks each piece—be it an Edwardian glove box or an Etruscan revival bracelet—with a poetic eye, and his finds often tell a winsome secret or a long-forgotten story. Unfortunately, the story of that porcelain wing is that it's not mine.

fort defiance

a great spot to get happily sated

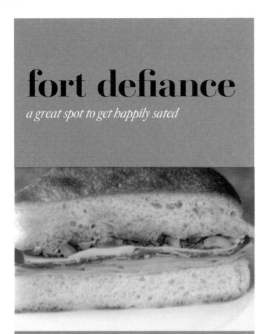

365 Van Brunt Street
Between Dikeman and Coffey
(Red Hook) *map E04*
Bus: 61/77
347.453.6672
www.fortdefiancebrooklyn.com

twitter @fortdefiance
sun - mon, wed - thu 8a - midnight
tue 8a - 3p fri - sat 8a - 2a
breakfast. lunch. dinner. brunch. full bar
$ first come, first served

Yes, Please: *vesper cocktail, journalist cocktail, muffaletta, deviled eggs, rabbit stroganoff, big braised pork shank, meatloaf sandwich, pimento cheese with ritz crackers*

CD: On the wide spectrum of modern-day cocktail connoisseurs, I'm somewhere in the middle. I'll geek out about bitters and gins and jiggers with the best of them, but in the end I believe a drink is a drink—it should have a few solid ingredients in it and be poured with care by a well-versed bartender. And I like to drink surrounded by happily sated folk. No other bar cum café cum restaurant personifies this philosophy better than **Fort Defiance**, where owner and expert hooch slinger St. John Frizell pours some of the best drinks around and always keeps it just this (right) side of real.

home/made
down-home wine bar

293 Van Brunt Street
Between Pioneer and King
(Red Hook) *map E05*
Bus: 61/77
347.223.4135
www.homemadebklyn.com

twitter @homemadebklyn
see website for hours
$-$$ first come, first served

Yes, Please: *brooklyn oenology "motley cru,"*
brundlmayer sekt brut, open-face smoked salmon with
chevre, warm potatoes provencal, charcuterie plate

CD: Some years ago, when I lived in Brooklyn, my boyfriend and I considered it a vacation to drive to Red Hook and spend the afternoon wandering the 'hood's scrubby streets and deserted docks. Back then there was nothing much to see, save for a few renegade art installations and an old coffee shop. Today, however, Van Brunt is lined with spots including **Home/Made**, a tiny eatery that feels more like a shabby chic living room than a restaurant. And when you're seated on one of the overstuffed couches, a glass of wine in hand, a savory tart on the way, the grubby urban frontier outside seems far away.

saipua

luscious soap and flower shop

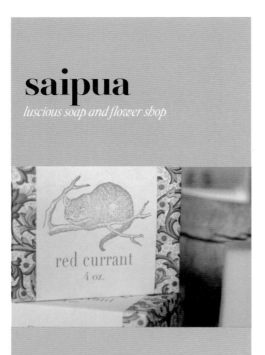

red currant
4 oz.

147 Van Dyke Street
Between Conover and Van Brunt
(Red Hook) *map S02*
Bus: 61/77
718.624.2929
www.saipua.com

twitter @saipua
sat - sun noon - 6p and by appointment
custom orders / design

Yes, Please: *soap: peppermint pumice, lemon geranium, saltwater exfoliating with nori , rosemary mint gardeners, mango butter; fresh flowers: peonies, daffodils*

CD: If my entire house looked and smelled like the tiny storefront that is Saipua, I would never leave. Part soap store, part floral shop, this place feels like an art installation set in an old barn. Except the "barn" is the size of a water closet and it's smack in the middle of Red Hook. **Saipua**'s handmade soaps are perched amid air plants and old twine, dried lavender, antique watering cans, and Mason jars. A dog is curled up on a floral chair. Peonies and poppies and daffodils sprout from corners and crannies. It's easy to fall in love with **Saipua**'s love of all things beautiful, innocent and pure.

brooklyn

boerum hill, cobble hill, carroll gardens

eat

shop

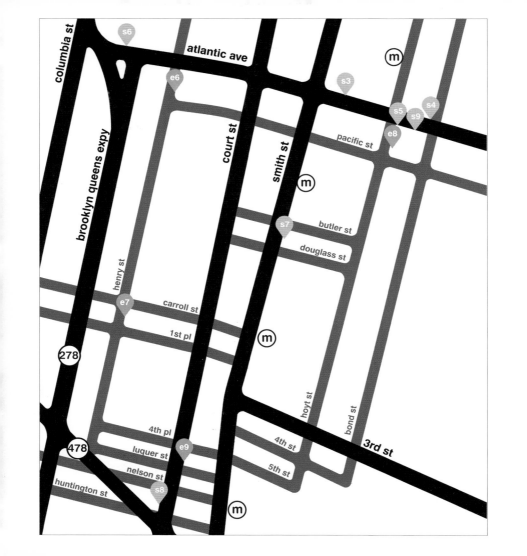

acorn

ultra tasteful goods for kids

323 Atlantic Avenue
Between Hoyt and Smith
(Boerum Hill) *map S03*
A/C/G: Hoyt-Schermerhorn
www.acorntoyshop.com

mon - wed 11a - 6p thu - sat 11a - 7p
sun noon - 6p
online shopping. registries

Yes. Please: *maileg of denmark rabbits, cuquito shoes, tamar mobiles, woven play, green elf toyworks, sandy vohr's leather goods, oeuf sweaters zoo, likeabike jumper*

JH: I attribute my affinity for design and finery to the fact that it was so absent in my rural Midwest upbringing. Starved for many years of anything extraordinary, I now go to great lengths to find the unique and refined. Perhaps the owners of the wonderful children's store **Acorn** were as deprived as I, because they have filled their shop with items of distinction and creativity. Better yet, these items are all for children. So never again will a child have to live with the bland and banal—that is if their parents are forward-thinking enough to shop at **Acorn**.

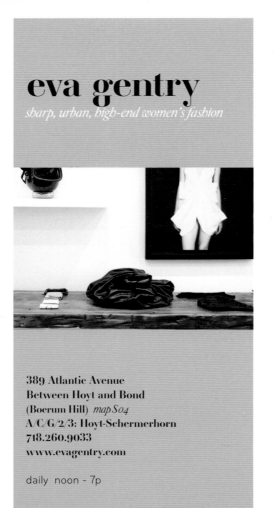

eva gentry
sharp, urban, high-end women's fashion

389 Atlantic Avenue
Between Hoyt and Bond
(Boerum Hill) *map S04*
A/C/G/2/3: Hoyt-Schermerhorn
718.260.9033
www.evagentry.com

daily noon - 7p

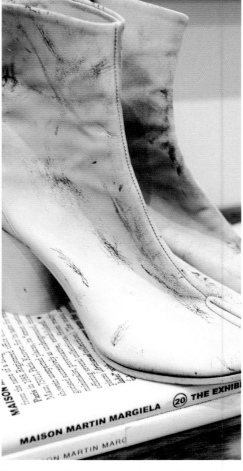

Yes, Please: *dries van noten, maison martin margiela, rick owens, guidi, michelle fantaci, dusan, gryson, eva gentry jewelry, m.a+, blk denim*

JH: You could easily say Eva Gentry offers the best selection of high-end women's designer clothing in Brooklyn. They sell lines rarely seen on the east side of the Brooklyn Bridge. But calling out Brooklyn somehow diminishes the excellence of this shop. It's akin to an award for Best in Show for dogs with white fur only. **Eva Gentry** has great clothing, and it happens to be located in Brooklyn. But there is more. In fact, just next door is their consignment store, which offers the same level of sharp, smart fashion but with more affordable price tags. A ha! A leg up.

henry public

eats and drinks with speakeasy ambiance

329 Henry Street
Between Atlantic and Pacific
(Cobble Hill) *map E06*
2/3/4: Borough Hall
718.852.8630
www.henrypublic.com

twitter @henrypublic
mon - thu 5p - 2a fri 5p - 4a
sat 11a - 4a sun 11a - 2a
dinner. full bar
$$ cash only. first come, first served

Yes, Please: *kings county sour cocktail, two-cents fancy cocktail, marrow bones with toast, grilled cheese with apple slices, turkey leg sandwich, juniper pickles*

JH: When times are flush in NYC, wallet-busting restaurants are all the rage. But when times are challenging, places start to harken back to the last great depression. A perfect example is **Henry Public**. Think of a Dixie-esque speakeasy serving killer cocktails and hearty burgers. Opened by the folks behind the popular Brooklyn Social, this crew knows how to create a place that's 100% authentic and full of vitality. With glimmers of hope on the economic horizon, 14k-gold-dusted sweetbreads will surely return. But **Henry Public** will continue to thrive. A happy upside to the economic downturn.

hollander & lexer

wearable fashions for men

358 Atlantic Avenue
Between Hoyt and Bond
(Boerum Hill) *map S05*
A/C/G/2: Hoyt-Schermerhorn
718.797.9190
www.hollanderandlexer.net

wed - sat 11a - 7p sun noon - 6p

Yes, Please: *hollander & lexer wool pants, barbour, alexander yamaguchi henleys, c.p. company, drakes knit tie, chronicles of never glasses, darr (h & l's sibling store)*

JH: Sometimes I look at men's fashion shows on Style.com and roll my eyes. I mean, really, what man is going to wear patent leather hot pants with a bat-wing, animal-print cardigan on top? It's entertaining but has nothing to do with the real world—unlike **Hollander & Lexer**, whose selection of labels and house brand are totally wearable and still fashionable. Not to mention that the store has an antique repair-shop-meets-industrial-shipyard kind of feeling. What could get more masculine than that? Believe me, it helps you feel butch when you sniff the Santa Maria Novella bath salts.

holler & squall

antiques and furnishings

71 Atlantic Avenue
Corner of Hicks (Boerum Hill) *map S06*
4/5: Borough Hall
347.405.3734
hollerandsquall.blogspot.com

thu - fri noon - 6p sat - sun 11a - 7p
custom orders

Yes, Please: *wooden cigar molds, bone alligator, hand-carved wooden race horse, wooden hat forms, candle snuffer/wick cutters, old metal card catalog*

JH: You would think my house would be exquisitely outfitted with the amount of shopping I am required to do for this job. It should be, but it isn't. Call it the cobbler's kid syndrome (i.e., the kid going barefoot). To get it up to snuff, I should buy a few of the goodies at **Holler & Squall**, and my humble abode would be nearly camera ready. The selection of carefully culled antiques and oddities is just what's needed to perk up my Ikea-centric living quarters. My problem now is deciding what to buy, and I'm going to kick myself if I make the wrong decision. Better buy it all.

lucali

handthrown brick oven pizza

575 Henry Street
Between Carroll and First
(Carroll Gardens) *map E07*
F/G: Carroll Street
718.858.4086

wed - mon 6 - 10p
dinner
$$ cash only. byob. first come, first served

Yes. Please: *calzones, pizzas; toppings include: artichoke hearts, basil, pepperoni, anchovies, garlic, home-made ricotta, portobello mushrooms*

JH: You never start praise with an apology, but here it goes anyway: I'm sorry that this photo of the uncommonly good pizza from Lucali isn't better. It really should make your mouth water and command you to have inappropriate pizza fantasies. But because we don't use flash and this atmospheric room is lit only by candles (they even cook by candlelight), the pic is a bit moody. Maybe I was distracted by the perfect crust, or the chew and char of the pie was so dreamy that I drifted into some Italian fantasy and didn't get the shot. Whatever my sad excuse, don't miss **Lucali**.

mile end

montreal jewish comfort food

97 Hoyt Street
Between Atlantic and Pacific
(Cobble Hill / Boerum Hill) *map E08*
A/C/G: Hoyt-Schermerhorn
718.852.7510
www.mileendbrooklyn.com

see website for hours
breakfast. lunch. dinner. brunch
$$ first come, first served

Yes, Please: *montreal bagel & shmear, pickle plate, hot borscht soup, poutine, roasted jerusalem artichokes, cured & smoked beef brisket with mustard on rye*

JO: What comes to mind when I say Jewish-French-Canadian? Paula Abdul's mother? Seth Rogan? No need to do a silly Internet search. The yummiest answer is **Mile End**. This cozy spot brings a taste of Montreal to Boerum Hill, thanks to the passion of co-owners Noah Bernamoff and Rae Cohen. Noah is from Montreal and met wife Rae there in college. Upon moving to NYC and Noah saying goodbye to a lawyer's life, they opened their first restaurant to share what they missed from up North—Montreal bagels (smaller, chewier than New York bagels), pickle plates and poutine. Oh yeah, and pastrami, which is their signature dish. Lucky us. Take that answer, Internet!

prime meats

it's all about the meat

465 Court Street
Corner of Luquer
(Carroll Gardens) *map E09*
F/G: Carroll Street
718.254.0327
www.frankspm.com

twitter @primemeats
see website for hours
breakfast. lunch. dinner. full bar
\$\$ reservations recommended

Yes. Please: *weinenstephan hefeweiss, landjäger,*
the vesper brett - alpine tasting board, 36 day dry-aged bone
in ribeye, herb & wild mushroom spätzle, linzer torte

JH: Meat is all the rage again! This is good news for us omnivores but less so for the relatives of my childhood pet cow, Big Buns, though I will say that times have improved for BB's ilk. All of this attention to meat and its provenance means the bovines of today are being raised in the best conditions and being fed the finest foods. At **Prime Meats**, the crack team behind the beloved Frankies Spuntino brings the same care and flair to the steakhouse concept but makes it interesting with a German/Austrian twist. Big Buns would be so proud.

smith + butler

heritage clothing for men and women, oh, and motorcycles

225 Smith Street
Corner of Butler (Cobble Hill) *map S07*
F/G: Bergen Street
718.855.4295
www.smithbutler.com

twitter @smithbutlerbk
see website for hours

Yes, Please: *barbour, unis, belstaff, tellason , makr, iro, billy kirk, pointer brand, will leather goods, brixton, seevees, penny stock, ace & jig*

JH: Ask any man or woman, gay or straight, to name the sexiest male movie stars of all time, and these names pop up: Paul Newman, Marlon Brando (*Streetcar*, not *Apocalypse*), James Dean, and Steve McQueen. These icons embodied American style. So why was there the Flashdance era? Or Pee-wee Herman's mini-suits? I thinks it's because we didn't have **Smith + Butler**, where old-school cool meets biker chic. Heritage brands like Pendleton and Pointer are sold alongside chic upstarts like The Hill-side. Hooray! It's okay to look brooding hot again, instead of like a malnourished whippet.

store 518

drool-worthy general store with a twist

518 Court Street
Between Nelson and Huntington
(Carroll Gardens) *map S08*
F/G: Smith Street
646.256.5041
www.store518.com

thu – sat noon – 8p sun 11a – 7p
online shopping (for butter dresses only)

Yes. Please: *butter by nadia tarr; antique rulers, necco wafers, vintage clogs, the illustrated human body, winnie the pooh bike, croquet set*

JH: Though this is not one of those "one-stop" shops where you can buy garden hoses and underwear simultaneously, **Store 518** does carry a little of everything: candy, antiques, curiosities, vintage and new clothing, and clogs! Opening a drawer in an antique pharmacy cabinet, you might find Necco wafers in one drawer, antique hairpins in another—some items are mouthwatering and others seriously drool-worthy. And not to be missed is owner Nadia Tarr's signature line of jersey dresses under the Butter label. One-stop shopping, no—but a shopping must, definitely.

the banquet

objects for the home and the body

360 Atlantic Avenue
Between Hoyt and Bond
(Boerum Hill) *mapS09*
A/C/G/2/3: Hoyt-Schermerhorn
718.522.6906
www.thebanquetnyc.com

twitter @thebanquetnyc
mon - fri noon - 7p sat 11a - 7p
sun noon - 6p
custom orders

Yes, Please: *plume jewelry: petite accordion chain,*
macrame trinket bib, knot rings; miranda bennett
collections: cake dress, pier dress; the banquet archive

JH: Collaborations can be tricky. We need look no further than Ozzy Osbourne and Miss Piggy's rendition of "Born to be Wild" to see how egos can get in the way of success. However, when a team is as good as it is at **The Banquet** (formerly Council), a collaboration can be greater than the sum of its parts. Here, each of the partners brings a different element of design to the table, with Pamela creating the jewelry and Miranda the clothing, both acting as curatorial voices in conjunction to the rest of the shopping story, which includes vintage furniture and vintage clothing and curiosities. It's a harmonious convergence.

brooklyn

park slope, prospect heights, clinton hill,
fort greene, bedford-stuyvesant

eat

beer table

artisanal beers and snacks

427b Seventh Avenue
Between 14th and 15th
(Park Slope) *map E10*
F: Seventh Avenue
718.965.1196
www.beertable.com

twitter @beertable
daily 5p - 1a
brunch sun noon - 5p
dinner. brunch. snacks
$$ first come, first served

Yes, Please: *piet-agoras, birra del borgo 25 dodici, ricotta with olive oil & bread, pickled eggs with jalepeño powder, schlenkerla pork sausage with salt potatoes*

JH: I've heard lardo, absinthe and small batch vodka all proclaimed as the next big (foodie) thing, to which my jaded mind thinks, "well, they're over."' Even though a lardo sandwich sounds worthy of angina, I prefer the classics. And it doesn't get more classic than beer. Or does it? At **Beer Table**, knowledge and conviction supplant hype with truly inspired nightly selections of esoteric beers. Owner Justin Philips expertly talked me through the list of taps, and I decided on a Piet-Agoras. It was hoppy and smooth, complex and unlike anything I've tasted before. I was hooked. Who needs hype when you've got the goods?

bklyn larder

glorious prepared foods, cheeses
and groceries

228 Flatbush Avenue
Between Bergen and Sixth
(Park Slope) *map E11*
2/3: Bergen Street
718.783.1250
www.bklynlarder.com

twitter @bklynlarder
mon - sat 10a - 9p sun 10a - 8p
grocery. light meals
$$ first come, first served

Yes, Please: *larder made: fresh pancetta, porchetta, rabbit*
rillettes, hams, squid salad, homemade almond butter,
roasted chickens, ice cream

BKLYN
LARDER

VERMONT
SHEPARD

RAW SHEEP'S MILK
PUTNEY, VT

$29 / LB

JH: As a kid, I would walk through our local Piggly Wiggly humming Peggy Lee's "Is That All There Is?" OK, I was a weird kid, but even at age 12 I knew there was potential for more in terms of groceries and food shopping. My tune changed recently. Literally a dream come true, **Bklyn Larder** sells top-notch, hand-chosen staples in the most beautiful environment. If the meats, cheeses or gelati aren't made in house, then you best believe they are the best on the market. I'm older now but still singing Peggy's tunes. **Bklyn Larder**, you give me a "Fever."

brooklyn flea

flea market food booths and much, much more

**Sat (Apr-Nov): 176 Lafayette Avenue
Between Vanderbilt and Clermont
(Fort Greene)** *map E12*
**Sun (Nov - Apr): 4 Hanson Place
Corner of Flatbush
All Trains: Atlantic Avenue / Pacific Street
www.brooklynflea.com
(See website for other locations)**

twitter @bkflea
sat - sun 10a - 5p
$-$$ mainly cash. first come, first served

Yes, Please: *salvatore ricotta, arugula & prosciutto bruschetta; asia dogs, sea bean goods, mcclure's pickles, fine & raw chocolates, liddabit brittle, brooklyn soda works*

CD: It was a simple smear of handmade ricotta that convinced Kaie and me to include **Brooklyn Flea** in this book. Part antique showcase, part outdoor gallery for local artisans and part food mecca, **Brooklyn Flea** looks and functions like a regular open air flea market, but it's the local cheese and chocolate makers, the taco slingers and pickle masters that really lend it cache. That ricotta? It was puffy and light, spread on a piece of bread, topped with arugula and prosciutto. After eating our way through the aisles, it was clear: this is where food-obsessed Brooklynites go to get sated.

dough

insanely addictive artisanal donuts

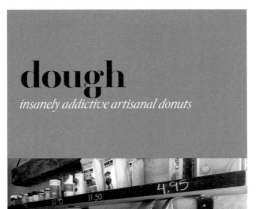

305 Franklin Avenue
Corner of Lafayette
(Fort Greene / Clinton Hill) *map E13*
G: Classon Avenue
347.533.7544

twitter @doughbrooklyn
daily 7a - 5p
treats. coffee / tea. grocery
$ cash only. first come, first served

Yes, Please: *donuts: blood orange with candied orange peel, dulce de leche, lemon meringue, hibiscus, cream cheese with graham cracker, chocolate with earl grey*

JO: Homer Simpson could not have chosen a better food to obsess over: Donuts. He and others with more self-restraint would no doubt take one look at the freshly glazed beauties offered at **Dough** and hand over the code to Springfield's nuclear warheads. There's nothing safe about these donuts. **Dough**'s inventive yet nostalgic flavor combos pull you in with their colors and then make you drool with their taste. Guard your military leaders. When I visited, there were two cops, three mothers, four too-cool-for-school teenagers, a pair of teachers and a couple of love birds. That's what makes **Dough** and its treats enjoyable—it's so egalitarian.

james

old-world euro meets seasonal american

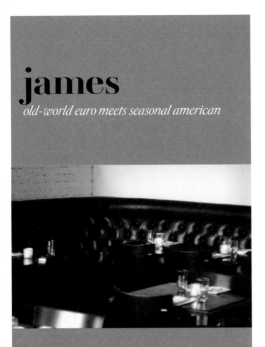

605 Carlton Avenue
Corner of St. Marks
(Prospect Heights) *map E14*
Q/B: Seventh Avenue > 3: Bergen Street
718.942.4255
www.jamesrestaurantny.com

dinner mon - sat 5:30 - 11p sun 5:30a - 10p
brunch sat -sun 11a - 3:30p
brunch. dinner. full bar
$$-$$$ first come, first served

Yes, Please: *st. anne's cocktail with st. germaine & basil,*
cauliflower soup with smoked sturgeon, sautéed skate with
"la ratte" potatoes, ricotta pancakes with stone fruit syrup

JFD: It's very in the mode these days to name an establishment after a grandparent. If a place annoys you, then this seems like a saccharine act. But if you really like a spot, then you'll embrace the sentimentality. The latter describes how I feel about **James**, named after the grandfather of chef Bryan Calvert. I don't know if the epony-mous James actually cooked this way—I know my grandparents boiled hot dogs, kept frozen Velveeta around and drank grapefruit juice out of a can—but that's why it's Bryan's restaurant and not mine. Sentimentality aside, the food here is what will make a memory.

no.7

not easily definable food

7 Greene Avenue
Corner of Fulton (Fort Greene) *map E15*
C: Lafayette
718.522.6370
www.no7restaurant.com

twitter @no7restaurant
see website for hours
lunch. dinner. brunch. full bar
$$-$$$ reservations accepted for parties
of six or more

Yes, Please: *mint sun tea with bourbon & lemon,
cold grilled octopus, pumpkin seed crusted tofu, chicken
stuffed cabbage, brown butter pudding*

KW: While I was at No.7, I spent some time chatting with Matt, one of the owners. I was being a bit cheeky when I asked why he and Tyler, the chef, didn't open a turn-of-the-century, Americana-esque spot. He gave me, rightfully so, the stink-eye, as these guys follow the beat of their own drum—which I heartily applaud. The food here is damn hard to categorize, but here's my stab: American meets Korean with a dash of Spanish flair. Most importantly, it's insanely delicious. And now there's **No.7 Sub** at The Ace Hotel, where their signature flair will be applied to the food du jour: sandwiches.

peaches

modern southern fare

393 Lewis Avenue
Between Macdonough and Decatur
(Bedford-Stuyvesant) *map E16*
A/C: Utica Avenue
718.942.4162
www.peachesbrooklyn.com

twitter @peachesbrooklyn
mon - thu 11a - 10p
fri - sat 11a - 11p sun 10a - 10p
lunch. brunch. dinner
$$ first come, first served

Yes, Please: *brownstone punch, harlem brewing sugar hill ale, market vegetable salad, turkey meatloaf sandwich, 12-hour smoked short ribs, wilklow farms country pies*

KW: A while back, my brother and I were discussing comfort food. He said his favorite was apples. Apples?? I'm still scratching my head over this. In my mind, comfort food is warm and filling and a little naughty. In my food vernacular, this means meatloaf, mac & cheese and pie—basically the food that is made at **Peaches**, but with an urban flair. I suggest sidling up to the bar where the über-charming Ron rules the roost. Have him pour you a brownstone punch and then dig into something homey, like the pulled pork and grits. If you're not comforted by the end of your meal, I'll eat my words.

roman's

fresh, cozy italian fare

243 Dekalb Avenue
Between Vanderbilt and Clermont
(Fort Greene) *map E17*
G: Clinton-Washington
718.622.5300
www.romansnyc.com

sun - thur 5 - 11p fri - sat 5p - midnight
brunch sat - sun 10a - 3:30p
dinner. full bar
$$-$$$ first come, first served

Yes. Please: *daily bitters, menabrea blonde, shaved hubbard squash with almonds & olives, pasta chitarra with tomato & raw cow cheese, sautéed tatsoi*

JFD: Rome wasn't built in a day, and **Roman's** didn't just spring forth in one day (nor did it emerge from a giant wolf). In fact, the owners cut their teeth on the imperative Williamsburg spots **Marlow & Sons** and **Diner**—a hop, skip and a BQE away—before creating this fresh Italian restaurant. But it's here now, and I'm happy to report that I veni, vidi, eati, drinki. Especially memorable was the chitarra: chewy, tender strips of pasta formed on a guitar-string frame and served with clean tomato sauce. Yum. Lend me your ears, countrymen, and let me suggest that you check out **Roman's**, too.

saraghina

*neapolitan pizza in a stylish,
vintage environment*

**435 Halsey Street
Corner of Lewis
(Bedford-Stuyvesant)** *map E18*
**C: Kingston-Throop
www.saraghinabrooklyn.com**

dinner daily 6 - 11p
breakfast and lunch mon - fri 10a - 5p
brunch sat - sun noon - 4p
$-$$ cash only. first come, first served

Yes, Please: *house red wine; pizzas: margherita, bufalo,
prosciutto & funghi, capocollo; burratina, tagliatelle al ragu*

AB: At the start of our work on this book, Jan and I were in the throes of distress and had a mutual bad case of the grumps. Then we went to **Saraghina**, and our attitudes took a turn for the better. Suddenly the world was golden and everything was wonderful. We were so taken by **Saraghina** and its divine pizza that we considered moving down the street in Bed-Stuy so we could commune daily with the regulars—from folks newly moved to the neighborhood to those who have spent their whole lives here. The mix was infectious, and the food was dee-lish-us.

brooklyn

williamsburg, bushwick

eat

shop

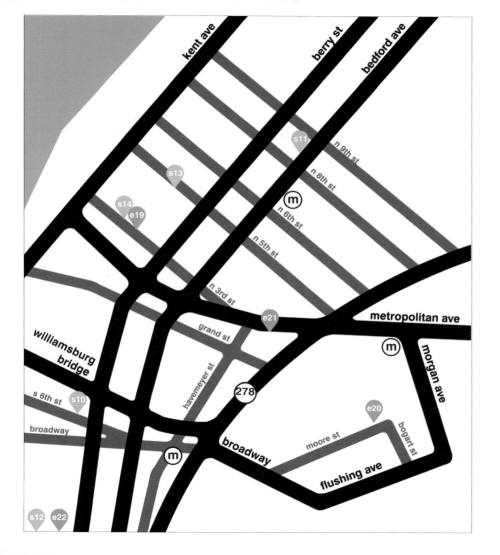

brook farm
general store

tasteful, useful stuff

75 South Sixth Street
Between Berry and Wythe
(Williamsburg) *map S10*
J/M/Z: Marcy Avenue > L: Bedford Avenue
718.388.8642
www.brookfarmgeneralstore.com

wed - mon noon - 7p
online shopping

Yes, Please: *tourne chun mee green tea, fog linen works*
leather key holders, anglepoise desk light, stanley flasks,
elementary screwdriver sets, japanese scrub brushes

KW: Though I like to think of myself as a kind and benevolent person, I think the authors of this book might describe me a little less kindly. Like Jon, whom I made tromp through a massive spring snowstorm to take a picture of a steak at **Prime Meats** and then traverse back to Williamsburg to visit **Brook Farm General Store** (if you read about somebody being mugged for his or her cross-country skis during this time, Jon was for sure the attacker). Though the journey here inspired a plentitude of !@!#, the experience at **Brook Farm** was nothing less than magical for Jon. A worthwhile place for which to journey.

jumelle

nicely edited collection of women's clothing

148 Bedford Avenue
Between Eighth and Ninth
(Williamsburg) *map S11*
L: Bedford Avenue
718.388.9525
www.shopjumelle.com

mon 1 - 7:30p   tue - sat noon - 7:30p
sun noon - 7p
online shopping

Yes. Please: *karen walker, isabel marant, bodkin, hope, mociun, aesa, cacharel, electric feathers, no. 6 clogs, conroy & wilcox, epice*

JFD: Little girls are warned by cluckish parents not to wear patent leather shoes because little boys might get a peek up their skirts in the reflection. Big girls, therefore, rush out to buy patent leather shoes. At least that's what I did. **Jumelle** had a perfect pair of patent loafers—a little pointy, very suave and polished to a blinding sheen. They would have paired perfectly with some of the equally enticing clothes that Candice Waldron selectively brings in. Modesty be damned—while I'm at it, I also want that Alexander Wang zipper-fronted dress. Let's see what the little boys make of that.

mast brothers chocolate

artisanal chocolate

**105A North Third Street
Between Berry and Wythe
(Williamsburg)** *map E19*
**L: Bedford Ave
718.388.2625
www.mastbrotherschocolate.com**

twitter @mastbrothers
mon - fri 3 - 7p sat - sun noon - 8p
treats
$ cash only. first come, first served

Yes, Please: *dark chocolate with black truffles & sea salt bar, dark chocolate with pecans & maple syrup bar, fleur de sel bar, cacao nibs, baking chocolate*

JFD: Have you ever seen a movie where the police stage a sting operation? They tell some dimwitted felons that they've won a big screen TV and tickets to a UFC cage match, and when the crooks show up to collect—it's slamma time. I've seen enough of these flicks that when I drew the coveted Williamsburg 'hood to cover for this book, meaning I'd get to visit **Mast Brothers**, I assumed I'd been set up. I mean, really? Handsome, musical, bearded men making artisanal, rigorously created and sourced chocolate in gorgeous packaging. Cuff me.

pomme

children's shop with french style

81 Washington Street
Between Front and York
(Dumbo) *map S12*
F: York Street
718.855.0623
www.pommenyc.com

twitter @pommenyc
tue - sun 11a - 7p

Yes, Please: *luco clothing, bon bon sweaters, atsuyo et akiko shirts & bags, petit pan balls, makié hats, the beatrix potter collection*

AB: The children in Paris always seem so beautifully dressed. If you spend a lazy Sunday afternoon in the Luxembourg Gardens watching the boys in their sweaters and slacks pushing their wooden boats in the pond and the girls twirling about in their pretty coats, it makes a storybook picture. Being at **Pomme** reminds me of those Parisian afternoons, as the clothing here looks like it could easily be a part of a Parisian's or New Yorker's, or just about any kid's wardrobe. Couple this with beautifully crafted toys and books and décor, and the **Pomme** picture is very pretty indeed.

roberta's
wood-fired pizza

261 Moore Street
Between White and Bogart Streets
(Bushwick) *map E20*
L: Morgan Avenue
718.417.1118
www.robertaspizza.com

twitter @robertaspizza
daily 11a - midnight
lunch. dinner. brunch. wine / beer
$$ first come, first served

Yes, Please: *fresh mint lemonade, juan benegas malbec, snapperhead ipa, romanesco salad with pistachio butter & lardo, good girl pizza, specken wolf pizza*

CD: Bushwick may be a trendy neighborhood in Brooklyn, but I still consider any business that opens up there a modern-day frontier outpost. Maybe it's the piles of firewood that greet you when you walk into **Roberta's** or the saloon-like feel of the bar or the fact that all the men have beards—but it feels pretty much like the Wild West. Of course there's the simplicity of the food to take into consideration—wood-fired pizzas, grilled skirt steak, roasted marrow bones—all of which makes this place the sort of joint I'd want to come upon after a long ride on the urban range.

saltie

*inventive sandwiches and market
fresh dishes*

ICE-CREAM.

CHOCOLATE
SALTIE CARAMEL
ANISE HYSSOP
LOAF   6
+
SCOOP 3
CAR BOMB! 4
ICE CREAM SANDWICH

378 Metropolitan Avenue
Between Marcy and Havemeyer
(Williamsburg) *map E21*
L: Bedford Avenue
718.387.4777
www.saltieny.com

twitter @saltieny
tue - sun 10a - 6p
breakfast. lunch. dinner. brunch
$-$$ cash only. first come, first served

Yes. Please: *plum cardamom lassi, aqua fresco;
sandwiches: scuttlebutt, ship's biscuit, clean slate, spanish
armada; eccles cake, ice cream sandwich*

JFD: Don't blame me if this whole blurb ends up in pirate speak. Blame the owners of **Saltie**. They're the ones who named the sandwiches "Scuttlebutt" and "The Captain's Daughter" and put up signage indicating "it's a tight ship" in this galley-sized take-out shop. But, avast, me hearty, if yar looking for sandwiches featurin' uncommon ingredients, in big heaps of bountiful freshness, set your compass for here. Actually, there's much more to this place than sandwiches, including scrumptious pastries and rich ice cream desserts. Landlubbers and food lovers welcome.

sweet
william

indie clothing for groovy kids

112 North Sixth Street
Between Berry and Wythe
(Williamsburg) *map S13*
L: Bedford Avenue
718.218.6946
www.sweetwilliamltd.com

mon - fri 11a - 7p sat - sun noon - 7p
online shopping. registries

Yes, Please: *talc, nico nico clothing, ada ada,*
nui organics, jess brown rag dolls, atsuyo et akiko, aigle boots,
hansa stuffed animals

JFD: Sweet, but with an urban edge. That's been the dressing code for the Phoebes, Sorens, Finns, Ellas, Hazels, and Rubys of the last ten years. **Sweet William** hits this balance just right, with clothing and toys that are eco-conscious but not precocious. Though most of my friends have settled down on the procreation front (as have I), I can imagine shopping here for the next round of kids to come, which, if my naming predictions hold, will be the Craigs and Brents, Brendas and Loris of the next decade. Naming cycles can be so cruel!

vinegar hill house

vintage ambiance and wood-fired cooking

72 Hudson Avenue
Between Front and Water Streets
(Vinegar Hill) *map E22*
F: York Street > A: High Street
718.522.1018
www.vinegarhillhouse.com

twitter @vinhillhouse
see website for hours
dinner. brunch. full bar
$$ first come, first served

Yes, Please: *highland cocktail, basque apple cider, oven-roasted octopus, pork rib cannelloni, cast-iron chicken, red wattle country chop, guinness chocolate cake*

JFD: I research long and hard before I ever set foot in a place, and then I research some more. Getting rid of the industry jargon, this means I eat and drink a lot. And I get giddy when my choices are validated. Sometimes this validation comes from within: the food is fantastic and I love the place. Sometimes the validation comes when I mention a restaurant to others whose judgment I trust, and they heartily concur. Other times it's because the press gushes in droves about the place. All of this is true of **Vinegar Hill House**. This city loves this restaurant, and I can validate the affection.

VOOS

showcase for nyc based furniture and product designers

105 North Third Street
Between Berry and Wythe
(Williamsburg) *map S14*
L: Bedford Ave
718.218.8666
www.voosfurniture.com

tue – sun noon – 6p
custom orders / design

Yes, Please: *desu design symbol coat rack, eskayel wall-papers, uhuru stoolen stools, by amt acrylic jewelry, laurie beckerman whistle lamp, design glut egg pants*

JFD: There is a hell of a lot of creativity, mirth and clever design going on in this ever-hopping neighborhood. But even with the bar set high, **Voos** will jolt the most jaded shopper. The furniture and décor here are crafted in unusual materials and take on unexpected forms—yet surprisingly nothing feels gimmicky or forced. Each little treasure is made and produced locally by NYC designers, hence the tagline "made here, feel good." I absolutely embrace that ethos, but I personally am not going to feel good until I bring one of these pieces home.

brooklyn

greenpoint

eat

shop

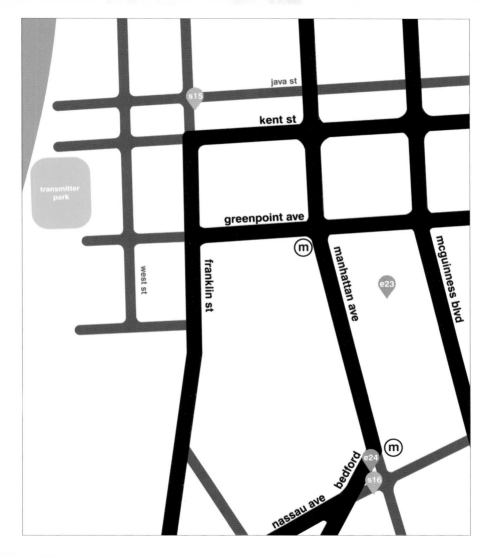

eat
greenpoint
healthy, local, seasonal food

124 Meserole Avenue
Between Leonard and Eckford
(Greenpoint) *map E23*
G: Nassau
718.389.8083
www.eatgreenpoint.com

twitter @eatgreenpoint
tues - sun noon - 10p
lunch. dinner. brunch. csa-share. byob
$$ cash only. first come, first served

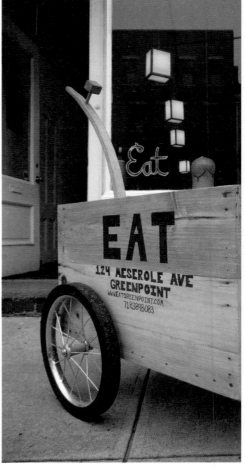

Yes, Please: *beet + cipollini onion soup, gnocchi with asparagus & stinging nettles, savory tart with herbs & greens, maple spelt cookies, hot nettle tea*

JO: Full disclosure here. My friend Toko cooks at **Eat** and she has always been a talent in the kitchen. So when she asked me to join her at this locavore spot, with the promise of truly regional food, I was out the door before she finished the text. **Eat** takes DIY to the next level. The handsome communal tables? They are built by owner Jordan Colón's brother, Jonathan. The beeswax candles? They are hand-dipped by the other brother, Seth, and sourced from the same bees that supply **Eat**'s honey. **Eat** even dries their own tea leaves (try the nettle). The three brothers Colón are helping create a kind of vegetable monastery. Not austere, but a sanctuary nonetheless.

kill devil hill

fine goods of all descriptions

170 Franklin Street
Between Kent and Java (Greenpoint) *map S15*
G: Greenpoint Avenue
347.534.3088

twitter @killdevilhill
mon - tue, thu - sat noon - 8p
sun noon - 6p
custom orders

Yes, Please: *b.s. mercantile cravats, b.s. mercantile custom pants , taxidermy beaver, antlers by the pound, brooklyn brine pickles, vintage coffee/tea kitten*

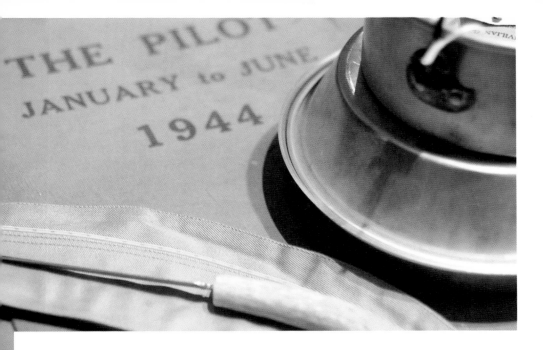

JH: I could never own a shop like Kill Devil Hill. Don't get me wrong—the shop's honky-tonk meets Appalachian backwoods antiques and objects are great. But if this were my place, I wouldn't be able to let go of anything. I would constantly second guess myself, convinced that *The Golden Girls* 20th anniversary plate should be priced extremely high due to its brilliance and popularity. As illustrated, I shouldn't be in retail. I'll leave it to those who have excellent taste, like owners Mark and Mary, and I'll stick to watching the GGs fight over the last piece of cheesecake.

loren

denim boutique and workshop

80 Nassau Avenue
Between Lorimer and Manhattan
(Greenpoint) *map S16*
G: Nassau
347.529.5771
www.lorencronk.com

thu noon - 6p fri 11a - 9p sat 11a - 8p
sun noon - 8p and by appointment
custom orders. repairs

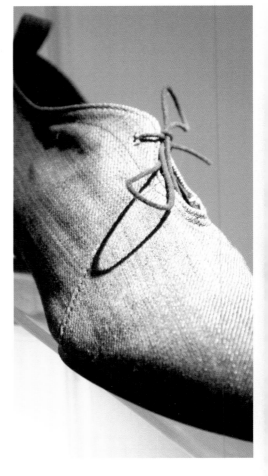

Yes, Please: *handmade custom jeans no. 81, blksmth regular roger jeans, soldier & brave high rise skinny fit, loren/keller denim shoe collabo, vintage belt buckle*

JO: What makes an extra good pair of jeans? One man, Loren Cronk, has devoted many hours at the sewing machine to find out. His namesake store also acts as his workspace—an atelier for the uniform of common sense, denim. **Loren** carries vintage jeans, but the real stars here are his own line of jeans. There's his handmade, one-of-a-kind custom orders, which he dries right in the store window. (He'd just completed No. 81 on my visit.) Then there's his affordable men/women's line, Soldier and Brave. And my personal favorite, his men's workwear line, Blksmth, which modernizes a classic cut. **Loren** will even repair your can't-let-'em-go jeans too.

van leeuwen artisan ice cream

ice cream and coffee worth searching for

**632 Manhattan Avenue
At Bedford and Nassau
(Greenpoint)** *map E24*
**G: Nassau > L: Bedford
See website for other storefronts and
truck locations
718.701.1630
www.vanleeuwenicecream.com**

twitter @ vlaic
see website for hours
coffee / tea. treats
$-$$ cash only. first come, first served

Yes, Please: *intelligentsia coffee, pastries & jellies;
ice creams: vanilla, chocolate, red currant, pistachio,
gianduja, ginger, strawberry, peppermint & chip*

JFD: I drove an ice cream truck during the summer in high school. I sped around trolling for kids, blasting Billy Idol in an effort to drown out the Joplin-esque calliope music. It was hell on earth. As you might imagine, I don't take too kindly to ice cream trucks. But **Van Leeuwen** charmed me. Concentrating on making just a handful of ice creams really well and turning out killer coffee, this family doesn't need to play foul jingles to attract (or repel) a crowd. The truck simply appears on certain Brooklyn and Manhattan street corners, and the people come. And since this book originally went on press, **Van Leeuwen** has opened not one, but three storefronts. Triple the pleasure.

queens

long island city, astoria, flushing

eat

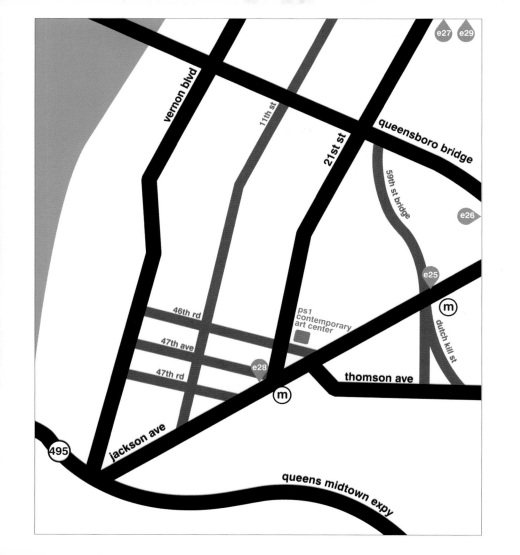

dutch kills

working man's cocktail bar

27-24 Jackson Avenue
Between Dutch Kills and Queens
(Long Island City) *map E25*
 N/W/Z/7: Queensboro Plaza
718.383.2724
www.dutchkillsbar.com

mon - sun 5p - 2a
full bar
$ first come, first served

Yes. Please: *bartender's choice, chin chin ,
st. charles punch, 1887 manhattan , archangel ,
gershwin, water lily, queens park swizzle*

CD: If I were a piano tuner at the Steinway factory in Long Island City, I'd go to **Dutch Kills** for an Old Fashioned after work. If I were a stevedore working on the docks, I'd buy my happy hour beer here. If I were a post-apocalyptic performance artist who just installed my video art at PS1 down the street, I'd come for an 1887 Manhattan to celebrate. And if I looked like Tom Waits, I'd bring my guitar, play it in the back, tap my cigarette ashes on the sawdust floor, and blend into the darkness. But while this is undoubtedly an everyman's bar, the cocktails are far from everyday. In fact, they transcend.

flushing, queens dumpling crawl

search for the ultimate chinese dumplings

PCS)	蜜棗粽子 SWEET RICE CAKE	$1.75/個(EACH)	STIR-FRIED RICE NOO... 酸辣湯 HOT & SOUR SOUP
CH)	茶葉蛋 TEA EGG	$1.00/3個(3PCS)	綠豆湯 GREEN BEAN SOUP
CH)	甜豆漿 SWEET SOYBEAN MILK	$1.50(大)(L) $0.75(小)(S)	銀耳湯 TREMELLA SOUP
CH)	咸豆漿 SALTY SOYBEAN MILK	$2.25(大)(L) $1.25(小)(S)	冷凍湯包 FROZEN SMALL B...
CH)	甜豆花	$2.50(大)(L)	各種冷凍... ALL KINDS FROZEN DU...

Spicy & Tasty: 39-07 Prince Street
Zhu Ji Guo Tie: 40-52 Main Street
Chinese-Korean Noodles & Dumplings:
133-31 39th Avenue (Flushing Mall)
(Flushing) *map E26*
7: Flushing Main Street

breakfast. lunch. dinner
$ first come, first served

Yes, Please: *favorite spots: spicy & tasty, zhu ji guo tie, chinese-korean noodles & dumplings*

JH: I came to Flushing with its amazing Chinatown to find the place with the best dumplings. This proved to be a hard job, as deciding between plump and meaty versus tender and delicate—or steamed rather than fried—sent me into a panic. Each dumpling I ate only further whet my appetite, making me want to continue my greedy search. Narrowing down to one favorite place seemed impossible. Then a carb-induced moment of inspiration happened. I decided to list all of my favorite spots and call this spread a dumpling crawl. Which was all I could do when I was done.

king of falafel & shawarma

unsurpassed middle eastern food cart

30th Street and Broadway
(Astoria) *map E27*
N/W: Broadway
718.838.8029
www.thekingfalafel.com

twitter @kingfalafel
mon – sat 11a – 9p
lunch. dinner
$ cash only. first come, first served

Yes. Please: *sodas, chicken & rice platter, falafel wrap, kefta sandwiches, chicken shish kabobs, lamb chops , shawarma hero, king mean platter*

JFD: It is, they say, good to be the king. It's also good to know the king. And if your path takes you by this fixture at 30th street in Astoria, you don't have a choice but to know the **King of Falafel & Shawarma**. Fares Zeidaies playfully calls out to all who pass by—mail carriers, working stiffs and loitering shifty characters. The smart ones head over and avail themselves of the intensely delicious food. The smartest customer I saw was the stroller-bound toddler who demanded his mother roll him over to the **King**. For his efforts, he got a fresh falafel. "He's a regular," King Fares told me. I'm not surprised.

manducatis

old-school italian

13-27 Jackson Avenue
Corner of 47th
(Long Island City) *map E28*
G: 21st Avenue
718.729.4602
www.manducatis.com

mon - fri noon - 3p, 5 - 10p
sat 5 - 11p sun 2:30 - 8p
lunch. dinner. full bar
$$-$$$ reservations accepted

Yes, Please: *negroni, espresso, octopus with chickpeas &
tomatoes, spaghetti with sun-dried tomatoes, pork chops
alla paesana, fettucine bolognese, cannoli*

CD: Call me a masochistic loon, but I like my Italian food cooked by stern Italian women and served to me by their slightly softer-edge Italian husbands. It's how the universe should work—which is why all is exactly as it should be at this near-ancient Long Island City haunt. Chef Ida Carbone cooks with a stone-cold poker face but a warm heart. Everyone in the room at **Manducatis**—and they've all been coming here for 20 years—knows Ida will cook the octopus to perfection and crank the spaghetti out herself. And if you order a Negroni from her husband Vincenzo? No need to worry about him scrimping on the gin.

philoxenia

tasteful greek dining

32-07 34th Avenue
Between 32nd and 33rd
(Astoria) *map E29*
N/W: Broadway

tue - fri 4 - 11p sat - sun 1 - 11p
dinner. full bar
$$ first come, first served

Yes. Please: *05 gaia estate assyrtiko, thalassitis, epirus, pan-fried graviera cheese, beets with skordalia, grilled bronzini, grilled shrimp with ladolemono dressing*

JFD: My only trip to Greece in the '90s yielded many firsts. My first time hitchhiking, eating whole fish, snorkeling, rapping the floor with my knuckles while shouting "opa!" and drinking retsina (okay, it was the first time I went to an Ikea also, but that's a random aside). With so many memorable firsts concentrated in one short visit, I've always felt a connection to the country. So now when I eat at a Greek restaurant, I want that connection validated by friendly, hospitable folk who will remind me of that amazing trip. That's exactly what I found at **Philoxenia**, along with whole fish and retsina. *Kalh orexh.*

manhattan

harlem, morningside heights

eat

e30 miss mamie's spoonbread too
e31 the hungarian pastry shop

shop

s17 swing: a concept shop

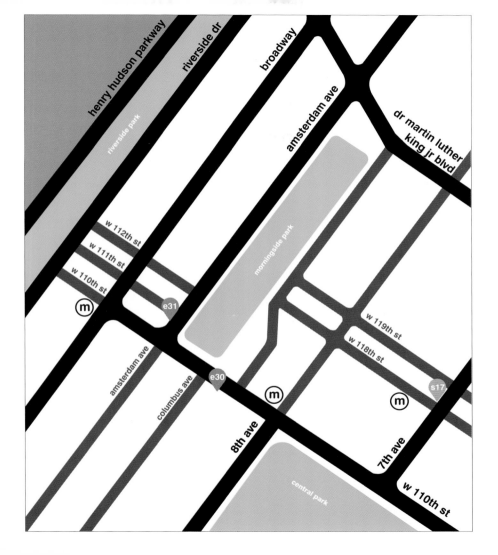

miss mamie's spoonbread too

southern cooking

366 West 110th Street
Between Columbus and Manhattan
(Harlem) *map E30*
B/C: Cathedral Parkway-110th Street
212.865.6744
www.spoonbreadinc.com/miss_mamies.htm

mon - thu noon - 9:30p
fri - sat noon - 10p sun 11a - 9:30p
brunch. lunch. dinner. wine / beer
$-$$ first come, first served

Yes. Please: *sweetened iced tea, harlem brewing company sugar hill golden ale, miss mamie's sampler, louisiana catfish, homemade meatloaf, hoppin' john, sweet potato pie*

CD: Fried chicken. Black-eyed peas. Collard greens. It's all at **Miss Mamie's**, and it's all very, very good. But it's made even better by the cheery green and yellow tiled floor. And the checkered tablecloths. And the red velvet cake perched on a glass cake stand, waiting for someone to slice into it. And the sunny disposition that **Miss Mamie's** embodies. Sure it's a little over the top, but after a day spent wandering the streets of Harlem and Morningside Heights, nothing feels more like coming home than digging into a plate of good old-fashioned Southern food. You're in good hands.

swing: a concept shop

signature clothing, iconic furniture and so much more

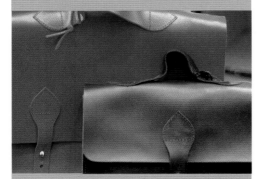

**1960 Adam Clayton Powell Jr Boulevard
Corner of 118th (Harlem)** *map S17*
**2/3/B/C: 116th Street
212.222.5802
www.swingaconceptshop.com**

twitter @swingharlem
mon, thu - sun 11a - 6p

Yes, Please: *ahene pa nkasa african bead necklace,
af vandervorst black pleated skirt, ann demeulemeester
georgia black silk dress, abstract mini ganesh*

CD: I'm generally suspicious of establishments that try to do too much. How could a store selling baby clothes, furniture, jewelry, men's and women's fashion, and tea really succeed? But somehow Helena Greene manages to curate her store so seamlessly you never once question her knack for diversification. Walking through the warm space, your eyes alight on a men's fedora, but then the smell of Kusmi tea turns your head, and then a basket of luscious silk scarves and wraps comes into view. It's a retail journey, and I enjoyed taking it.

the hungarian pastry shop

old-world bakery and café

1030 Amsterdam Avenue
Between 110th and 111th
(Morningside Heights) *map E31*
1: Cathedral Pkwy-110th Street
212.866.4230

mon - fri 8a - 11p sat 8:30a - 11:30p
sun 8:30a - 10:30p
treats
$ cash only. first come, first served

IN CASE OF FI
Keep Calm
Pay Bill
Then Run

Yes, Please: *cappuccino, viennese coffee, marzipan cake, seven-layer pyramid cake, rigo jancsi chocolate cake, sacher torte, cherry & cheese strudel, dobos torte*

CD: The first time I visited Europe, I didn't go to France or Italy. I went to Hungary on a work trip. And though it had never crossed my mind to travel there, I fell deeply in love with the place, in large part because of the dobos torte—a luscious five-layer sponge cake interspersed with chocolate buttercream and crunchy caramel—served in just about every café in Budapest. Though **The Hungarian Pastry Shop** is much more rustic than the opulent dessert shops of Budapest, eating the dobos torte at this funky, old-world spot felt just as luxurious.

manhattan

upper west side, upper east side

eat

café sabarsky

elegant spot for a viennese lunch and pastries

1048 Fifth Avenue
Corner of 86th (Upper East Side) *map E32*
4/5/6: 86th Street
212.288.0665
www.cafesabarsky.com

mon 9a - 6p wed 9a - 6p
thu - sun 9a - 9p
breakfast. lunch. dinner. coffee / tea
$$-$$$ first come, first served

Yes, Please: *06 sauvignon blanc steinmühle, kaiser mélange, speck with melon & mustard-pickles, chestnut soup with armagnac prunes, klimttorte mit schlag*

JH: The reason to put up with sky-high rents and rat-filled subways in New York, in my humble opinion, is the proximity to grandeur. Why do you think Grand Central Station got its name? Because it's not in Peoria. Another example of grand elegance in this city is lunch at **Café Sabarsky**. Attached to the Neue Gallery of Art in a former Vanderbilt mansion, it can't help but give you an "I'm not in Kansas anymore" reaction. It's the walnut-paneled room and the proximity to priceless Schieles that make the whipped cream that much richer and the klimttorte that much more decadent.

dovetail

humble three-star restaurant

103 West 77th Street
Between Columbus and Amsterdam
(Upper West Side) *map E33*
1: 79th Street > B/C: 81st Street
212.362.3800
www.dovetailnyc.com

see website for hours
lunch, dinner. brunch
$$$ reservations recommended

Yes. Please: *d'groni cocktail, lamb's tongue muffaletta presse with olives & capers; halibut confit with cabbage, quail egg, truffles; chamomile panna cotta*

CD: It's hard to believe that any neighborhood in this vibrant city could be considered the veritable equivalent of milquetoast, but the Upper West Side has this reputation, especially when it comes to dining. That is until **Dovetail** showed up on the scene with chef John Fraser's playful new American cuisine. Though the décor is a bit bland, the menu is full of bright spots. A chestnut soup sprinkled with pumpernickel croutons, currants and garnished with a luxurious foie gras cream? Yes. Kumamoto oysters suspended in cucumber sauce with American caviar? No milquetoast here.

lexington candy shop

old school, yummy lunch counter

1226 Lexington Avenue
Corner of 83rd (Upper East Side) *map E34*
4/5/6: 86th Street
212.288.0057
www.lexingtoncandyshop.com

twitter @lexingtoncandy
mon - sat 7a - 7p sun 8a - 6p
lunch. dinner. treats
$-$$ first come, first served

Yes, Please: *fresh lime rickey, egg creams, cherry coke float, shrimp salad platter, fried egg sandwich, liverwurst sandwich, butterscotch sundae, miss gimble's cheesecake*

JH: At the risk of sounding cliché, I'll say that **Lexington Candy Shop** is exactly what a New York City lunch counter should be. Diners sit on stools or in booths. Devil's food cakes are displayed on stands. The food is totally unfussy and satisfying. There are good ol' tuna melts, or if you're intent on dieting, try the '70s version of the South Beach Diet: a hamburger patty with cottage cheese and a lettuce leaf on the side. I was starting to wax nostalgic here, humming old standards by the Andrews Sisters when my waitress said, "Do you want another egg cream, sugar?" Whoa! Happy days are here again!

manhattan

midtown, murray hill, gramercy park

eat

shop

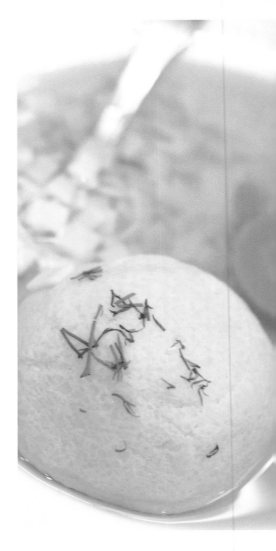

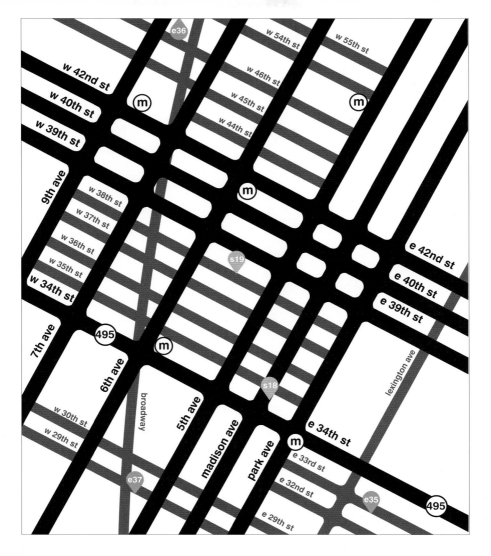

2nd avenue deli

a beloved jewish deli

162 East 33rd Street
Between Lexington and Third
(Murray Hill / Gramercy Park) *map E35*
5/6: Third Avenue
See website for second location
212.689.9000
www.2ndavedeli.com

sun - thu 6a - midnight fri - sat 6a - 4a
breakfast. lunch. dinner
$-$$ first come, first served

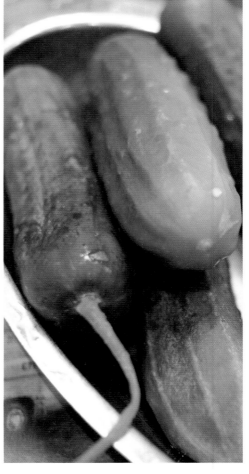

Yes, Please: *dr. brown's cel-ray soda, bosco & soda, chopped liver, matzoh ball soup, meat & potato knish, hot pastrami sandwich, gefilte fish, rugalach*

KW: Never in the history of doing these books have I ever had as much fun as I had eating lunch at **2nd Avenue Deli**. From the moment I walked in here, Mo and Karen and Steve took me under their wing. Soon I was sitting at the counter with a big bowl of matzoh ball soup kvetching away with my countermates Morton and Jordi. Plates and plates of food kept appearing before me like I had a Jewish fairy grandmother whipping things up in the kitchen. I truly died and went to kosher deli heaven. By the time I left, hours later, hugs were in order. I love this place.

complete traveller antiquarian bookstore

vintage travel books and maps

199 Madison Avenue
Corner of 35th
(Murray Hill / Grammercy Park) *map S18*
6: 33rd Street
212.685.9007
www.ctrarebooks.com

mon - fri 9:30a - 6:30p sat 10a - 6p
sun noon - 5p
online shopping

Yes, Please: *wpa american guides, baedeker guides, panorama guides, tibet & nepal by a. henry savage landor, le tour du monde en velocipede*

KW: What do I do for a living? I'm the publisher of a series of travel guides. So you would think I might have a deep knowledge of the history of this publishing genre. Insert sound of gong here. Sadly, I had never seen a Baedeker guide until I entered the **Complete Traveller**. Just so you don't think I'm a complete numbskull, I do collect other guides from all over the world, but none more than about 15 years old. Here there are guides, travel writings and maps that were published toward the beginning of the 20th century. This is what you call having a good shelf life.

danji

modern korean cuisine

346 West 52nd Street
Between Eighth and Ninth
(Midtown Westside) *map E36*
C/E: 50th street
212.586.2880
www.danjinyc.com

twitter @danjinyc
lunch. dinner. full bar
$$ reservations accepted for parties of
six or more

Yes, Please: *"tokyo drift" cocktail, spicy korean fire chicken wings, poached sablefish with spicy daikon, pork belly sliders, steak tartare, kimchi tofu*

JO: Hooni Kim, the chef and owner of Danji, has a theory: Korean food in the United States hasn't evolved in thirty years. This is not a derisive statement—it feels more like a personal goal to bring his vision of his nation's cuisine to more modern times by staying true to the flavors of real Korean food but using organic ingredients from mindful and sustainable farming operations. This is a place where the diner will even know where the kimchi comes from... Chef Hooni's mother-in-law! As a fellow Korean-American, I couldn't be more excited about this talented chef both challenging and honoring traditions. We all need a push to new places, and **Danji** is here to make it a belly-grinning ride.

hyman hendler & sons

third generation ribbon store

21 West 38th Street
Between Fifth and Sixth
(Midtown Westside) *map S19*
B/D/F/V: Bryant Park
212.840.8393
www.hymanhendler.com

mon - fri 9a - 5p
online shopping

Yes, Please: *mackintosh scarves, velvet ribbon, ultra-wide grosgrains, vintage jacquards, luxurious 76 satins, royalty picot taffeta, velvet plaids*

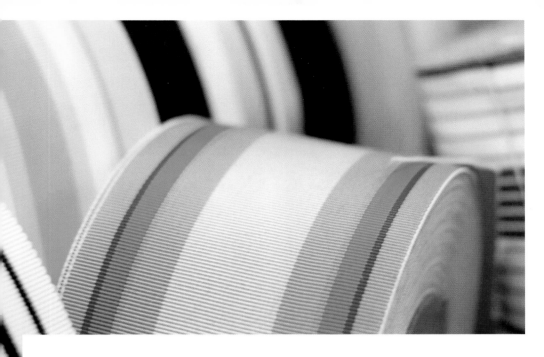

JH: Ribbon stores seem like something out of the past. Their heyday evokes a time when people either made their own clothes or needed an adornment to perk up a droopy mood. This notion seems positively Depression era, so how can a ribbon store make it today? Hmmm. What's old is new again? What goes around comes around? I certainly see a lot of droopy moods needing a little pick-me-up. **Hyman Hendler** is a ribbon wonderland that's seen good times and bad times—always focusing on supplying incredible ribbon. And without a government bailout either.

the breslin

high-end english pub fare

16 West 29th Street (In the Ace Hotel)
Between Broadway and Fifth
(Murray Hill / Gramercy Park) *map E37*
R/W: 28th Street
212.679.1939
www.thebreslin.com

twitter @thebreslin
see website for hours
breakfast. lunch. dinner. full bar
$$-$$$ first come, first served

Yes, Please: *the breslin bloody mary, hot cross buns, full english breakfast, blood sausage with eggs & creamy tarragon, beef & stilton pie, eton mess*

JFD: Location, location, location. **The Breslin** is situated in a confluence of neighborhoods, where Gramercy Park begins to meet the Flatiron District. But that's not the location I speak of. **The Breslin** can also be located directly below your bed, as it's situated on the ground floor of the of-the-moment Ace Hotel. You need only hail an elevator to experience April Bloomfield's British haute comfort food that honors "nose-to-tail" thinking. Staycation is still a goofy word, but if this spot—with its UK provenance by way of the Pacific Northwest, as interpreted in New York style—is your destination, well then what a great itinerary.

manhattan

*west village, greenwich village, chelsea,
meatpacking district*

eat

shop

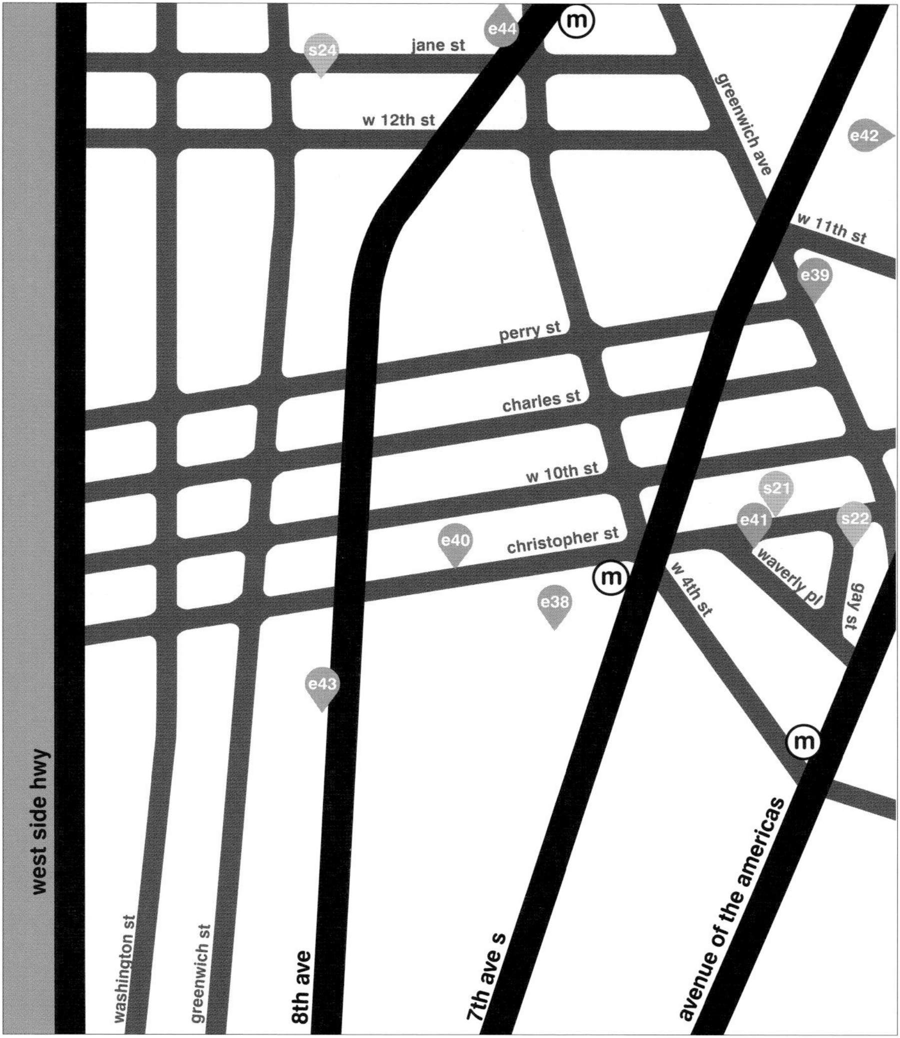

jane st
w 12th st
greenwich ave
w 11th st
perry st
charles st
w 10th st
christopher st
waverly pl
gay st
w 4th st
west side hwy
washington st
greenwich st
8th ave
7th ave s
avenue of the americas
m
m
m
m
s24
e44
e42
e39
s21
e41
s22
e40
e38
e43

buvette
the best french gastroteque

42 Grove Street
Between Bedford and Bleecker
(West Village) *map E38*
1: Christopher Street
212.255.3590
www.ilovebuvette.com

twitter @ilovebuvette
mon - fri 8a - 2a sat - sun 4p - 2a
breakfast. lunch. dinner. brunch
light meals. coffee / tea. treats
$$ first come, first served

PÂTISSERIE 5.

CROISSANTS
with butter & raspberry jam
SCONES
whole wheat currant scones
SPOON BREAD
t bread w/ sweet crème fraîche

FLES & CREPES 10.

BELGIAN WAFFLE
topped with strawberries
CREPES NUTELLA
hazelnut chocolate crepes
S JAMBON FROMAGE
baked with ham & bre

STRAWBERRIES - MUSELI - YOGURT FRESH FRUIT

7. TARTINES

WALNUT CRANBERRY BREA
farmers cheese, honey & bee pollen
NUTELLA & RICOTTA
nutella & sheep's milk ricotta
BEURRE au MARMALADE
orange marmalade & whipped butter

12. OEUFS

STEAMED
scrambled with prosciutto or smoked salmo
POACHES
poached egg over escarole, fava with pecori
FRITS à l'AMÉRICAINE
sunny-side eggs with house-cured pork belly

Yes. Please: *martini, kir royale, bloody mary, lemonade/*
lemonari/lemonice, croque mademoiselle, charcuterie,
fromages, brandade, pâté, tart tatin, chocolate glace

JO: Jody Williams loves to cook. And **Buvette** embodies that love, *mes amours*. The word *buvette* in French means a neighborhood refreshment stand, and boy does Jody's new spot live up to that phrase. It's open from 8am to 2am during weekdays, thus allowing you to come in for an *ouef* or *tartine* while you read the morning paper, then stay for a *croque mademoiselle*, whereupon you'll meet up with friends and slip on to a chilled martini. That'll work up your appetite again to eat some more! By midnight you'll still be happy, laughing through a soft chocolate pudding and falling in love. *Merde*. What a lovely way to spend your day.

gottino

enoteca e salumeria

52 Greenwich Avenue
Between Sixth and Seventh
(West Village) *map E39*
1/2/3: 14th Street
212.633.2590
www.ilmiogottino.com

twitter @gottinonyc
mon - fri 8a - 2a sat - sun 10a - 2a
breakfast. lunch. dinner
$$ first come, first served

Yes, Please: *07 ribolla gialla petrucco, carciofi e mentuccia crostini, braised rabbit pot pie , olive oil whipped house cured salt cod, nutella & toast*

AB: If I wasn't addicted to good food before, eating at **Gottino** solidified my position as a diehard lover of all things edible. I should clarify though. If food looks and tastes like cardboard and glue, then (obviously) I couldn't care less about it. But when food is both delicious and beautiful to look at, as it is at **Gottino**, I am 100% committed. At this place even a simple piece of toast is transformed into a piece of edible art. As for saying anything else here with words, I'm going to hold off and let the pictures do the talking.

greenwich letterpress

letterpress card shop

39 Christopher Street
Between Sixth and Seventh
(Greenwich Village) *map S20*
1: Christopher Street
212.989.7464
www.greenwichletterpress.com

twitter @greenwichlpress
tue - fri 11a - 7p sat - sun noon - 6p
online shopping. custom orders / design

Yes, Please: *custom greenwich letterpress products, nikki mcclure things to make & do, enormous champion letterpress whale cards, pop culture pencils, woodgrain bookplates*

AB: I just started taking a letterpress class, which has more than doubled my already high and glowing view of the craft. Metal typefaces, hand-setting type, learning the tricks and techniques of how to lay out and print—all of this strikes me as I look at the beautiful cards and paper products on display at **Greenwich Letterpress**. While I am excited to say I just hand-set my first line of type, spelling out my name in proud Copperplate Bold, I don't plan on giving up my paper store obsession anytime soon. **Greenwich Letterpress** is a habit I have no desire to break.

i sodi

authentic italian

105 Christopher Street
Between Bleecker and Hudson
(Greenwich Village) *map E40*
1: Christopher Street
212.414.5774
www.isodinyc.com

daily 5:30 - 11p
dinner
$$-$$$ reservations recommended

Yes, Please: *negroni, pasta & ceci minestre, lasagne ai carciofi , lasagne al sugo di carne, tortelli burro & salvia, galletto schiacciato, branzino alla griglia con fagioli*

AB: Some people are hardwired to dig deeper and work harder, and because of this, their creative output out-shines almost everybody else's. Rita Sodi is one of these types, and people flock to her eponymous restaurant, **I Sodi**, like it's the North Star. From the olive oil she hand presses from the trees on her property in Tuscany to the fresh pasta she rolls out daily—it is clear that this is a person who truly cares about the food she serves to her devoted and hungry followers. I can say that the lasagna I had here was the best I've ever eaten, and I will beat a path to **I Sodi**'s door every chance I get.

joseph leonard

crushable american "brasserie" cuisine

170 Waverly Place
Corner of Grove
(Greenwich Village) *map E41*
1: Christopher Street
646.429.8383
www.josephleonard.com

see website for hours
lunch. dinner. brunch. full bar
$$-$$$ first come, first served

Yes, Please: *rye tea cocktail, professor bucky, frisee & lardon, warm bean salad, pastrami sandwich, roast chicken for two, warm brownie*

AB: For every book that I've authored, there's always one place that I can't get out of my mind. Joseph Leonard is this place in this book. I liken my experience here to a really great first date. At the initial meeting, I felt pure (okay, it was lustful) attraction. As the date progressed, I relaxed and was soon besotted by the utterly warm yet non-smarmy charm of my companion. By the end of the date I was absolutely sure that **Joseph Leonard** was "the one." Now my only worry is how many other people have also fallen for **Joseph**, as I don't know if I can share. My love feelings I'm sure will also extend to **Joseph's** new sibling, **Fedora**.

leffot

exquisitely crafted men's shoes

10 Christopher Street
Between Sixth and Seventh
(Greenwich Village) *map S21*
1: Christopher Street
All Lines: West Fourth Street
212.989.4577
www.leffot.com

twitter @leffot
mon - sat 11a - 7p sun noon - 6p

Yes, Please: *shoes: church, gaziano, edward green, alden, rider boot co., danner, made-to-order pairs; ephtee trunks handmade in france, polishing leather map*

AB: My grandfather's shoe size is 15. My grandmother wore a size 8. When they traveled the world, she packed her shoes inside of his to protect them and save space. To this day, when I see gorgeously made men's shoes, I can't help but think of my grandmother nestling her elegant Ferragamos inside my grandfather's battleships. He would have been well served by some of the exquisitely crafted shoes found at **Leffot**. And now that they carry a small selection of women's shoes also, I can imagine what my grandmother would have chosen. Or even better, what I will choose.

num pang

cambodian sandwiches

21 East 12th Street
Between 5th and University
(Greenwich Village) *map E42*
All lines: 14th-Union Square
See website for other locations
212.255.3271
www.numpangnyc.com

twitter @numpang
mon – sat 11a - 10p sun noon - 9p
lunch. dinner. light meals
$ cash only. first come, first served

Yes. Please: *blood orange lemonade; sammies: peppercorn catfish, coconut tiger shrimp, five spiced pork belly, roasted salt & pepper japanese yam; grilled corn on the cob*

MI: Whether visiting New York or just surviving it, some days you need sustenance, quickly and deliciously. Quality is usually the first thing to get the boot... unless you're within walking distance of the two **Num Pang Sandwich Shops**. A tiny cash-only spot with a walk-up window and a few seats upstairs, **Num Pang** serves the perfect post-work, pre-commute, mid-day Cambodian-American sammie. I'm actually not sure how these differ from the trendy Vietnamese *bahn mi* sandwiches you find elsewhere, but I do know that a take-home meal of **Num Pang** watermelon juice, grilled corn on the cob, and a toasted Parisi baguette stuffed with juicy coconut-shrimp, chili mayo, pickled veggies, and cilantro... is like eating a vacation! *Muah*!

takashi

japanese/korean grill-it meat mecca

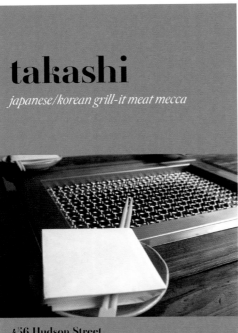

456 Hudson Street
Between Barrow and Morton
(West Village) *map E43*
1: Christopher Street
212.414.2929
www.takashinyc.com

twitter @takashinyc
mon - thu 6 - 11p fri 6 - 11:30p
sat 5:30p - 11:30p sun 5:30 - 10:30p
dinner. wine / beer only
$$-$$$ reservations accepted for parties
of four or more

Yes, Please: *beef shmaltz crostini , yooke (chuck eye tartare with raw quail egg and special sauce), niku uni (chuck flap, sea urchin and fresh wasabi), kalbi (shortribs)*

JO: The illustrated mural inside Takashi will lead you on a hilarious guided tour to the health benefits of eating meat. You'll also learn the difference in taste and texture of, say, the fourth stomach vs. the first and why too much flipping during grill-time is a big no-no. Yes, that's right, this place encourages participation. But chef/owner Takashi makes it so tasty and easy. He's already sourced the highest quality meat and marinated it two ways (your choice)—now all you need to do is grill and flip. Hooray for drool-worthy high-end grilling!

the crangi family project

some robust, some whimsical metal jewelry

212.929.0858
www.crangifamilyproject.com
www.gilesandbrother.com

online shopping

Yes, Please: *crangi line: mara, forged, venetian; giles & brother line: book with leather lashing bracelet; pied-de-biche rings, rings & nuts necklace*

JFD: Some buy lottery tickets—I prowl the semi-annual student art sale at the Rhode Island School of Design. Someday, I figure, I'll be buying the early work of the next Chihuly or Shepard Fairey. I'm annoyed, though, that I didn't pick up a piece of RISD alum Philip Crangi's jewelry. This absurdly talented jeweler and his sister Courtney make pieces that can range from delicate and sweet to steampunk and aggressive. Though I'm disappointed I didn't discover Philip early on, at least I can start collecting his pieces now at **The Crangi Family Project** website while I wait for their new storefront to open, hopefully soon!

txikito

cocina vasca

240 Ninth Avenue
Between 24th and 25th (Chelsea) *map E44*
C/E: 23rd Avenue
212.242.4730
www.txikitonyc.com

twitter @txikitonyc
see website for hours
lunch. dinner. brunch
$$ first come, first served

Yes, Please: *farnum hill "basque-style" cider, elkano cocktail, patatak, txiki txanpi, arraultza, pulpo, morcilla, esparragos, txilindron*

KW: When I lived in Chelsea during my college years, I used to think that the little retail strip on Ninth Avenue near 23rd would be a great place for a restaurant. Twenty or so years later, the folks at **Txikito** saw the same promise and planted their Basque roots here (as did Jim Lahey, whose great pizza spot **Co.** is on the corner). So I sat myself at the bar and proceeded to order paper thin slices of octopus and triangles of breaded tongue with cornichons. After eating I felt slightly depressed. The food was incredibly good, but what a downer that I no longer lived in this neighborhood so I could eat here every night and visit their tiny sister spot, **El Quinto Pino**, across the street.

zero + maria cornejo

a designer's atelier

807 Greenwich Street
Corner of Jane
(West Village) *map S23*
6: Bleecker Street
212.620.0460
www.zeromariacornejo.com

mon - sat 11a - 7p sun noon - 6p

Yes, Please: *zero + maria cornejo: little o dress, spiral dress, off kilter swing dress, kiba dress, koya coat, fur concave coat, fela boot; men's clothing*

AB: There are a few outfits in my life that stick out in my mind. First, the Heinz Ketchup Halloween outfit I wore, age 10, with my best friend who donned a matching mustard get-up. Second, my wedding dress. And third, a **Zero + Maria Cornejo** dress I borrowed from my sister. It was my first exposure to the line, and ever since, I have been an adoring fan. While taking photographs for this book, I could barely contain myself to stay on track and stick to the job at hand because all I wanted to do was drop the damn camera and try everything on. There's a lifetime of memorable clothing to be had here.

manhattan

soho, noho, nolita, little italy

eat

shop

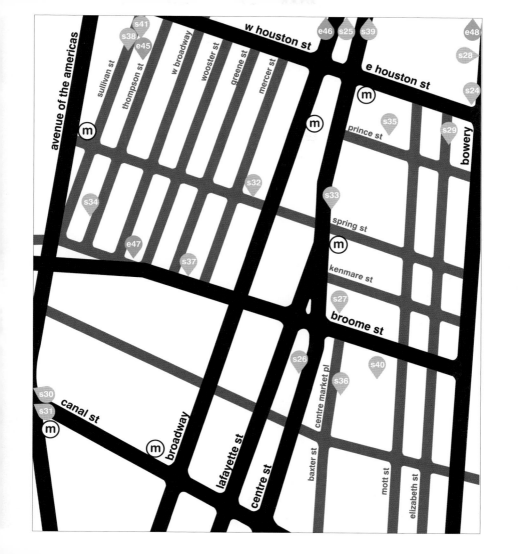

birdbath
bakery

neighborhood green bakery

160 Prince Street
Between Thompson and West Broadway
(Soho) *map E45*
C/E: Spring Street
See website for more locations
212.612.3066
www.thecitybakery.com/birdbath

twitter @birdbathbakery
mon - fri 8a - 7p sat 9a - 7p
sun 10a - 7p
$ first come, first served

Yes. Please: *farmer's lemonade, ronnybrook farm milks, pretzel croissant, housemade granola, blueberry honey scone, crazy good cookies, leek pizza with scallion & mint*

JFD: As predictable as swallows to Capistrano, I return to **Birdbath Bakery** whenever I come to town. My powerful homing instincts tell me that here, in this little nest of a bakery (in the old **Vesuvio Bakery** space), I'll find refuge from the bustling streets outside. More importantly, I'll find the sustenance required to power any other flights around the city I might have planned. I can't help but sing loudly the praises of their giant cookies, buttery pastries and inventive sandwiches. And no worries about a Silent Spring on account of **Birdbath**; the bakery employs truly green and sustainable practices. Make sure it's on your migratory path.

b-4 it was cool
industrial antiques

89 East Houston Street
Corner of Bowery (Nolita) *map S24*
F/V: Second Avenue
B/D/F/V: Broadway-Lafayette
212.219.0139
www.b4itwascool.com

daily noon - 7p

Yes, Please: *vintage: dental lights, toledo stools, american industrial lights, holophane lights, zafira fan, bakelite ribbon fan, tadpole model*

KW: I know there's been a downturn in this city, like everywhere else in the world, but I sincerely doubt that Gadi Gilan has felt it at his seminal industrial antiques outpost, **B-4 It Was Cool**. The reason? Because the à la mode style in restaurant and retail design—not just in NYC but across the country—is early Americana. Fixturing that speaks of the first 40 years or so of last century is sooooo of this century, and Gadi has stockpiles of it. Though lighting is the star here, there's also a plethora of stools, fans and some other ephemera thrown in for good measure. If you need a loan, ask Gadi for one.

c'h'c'm

expertly curated casual menswear classics

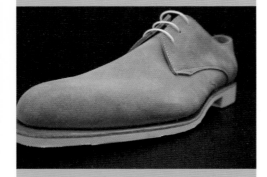

2 Bond Street
Between Broadway and Lafayette
(Nolita) *map S25*
B/D/F/M: Broadway - Lafayette
6: Bleecker
212.673.8601
www.chcmshop.com

twitter @chcmshop
daily 11a - 7p
online shopping

Yes, Please: *paraboot 'sanary' tan suede shoes, sunspel french stripe one pocket t-shirt, mackintosh kellas, chauncey pullover, stitchandsew canvas backpack*

JO: Sweetu Patel named his thoughtful, well-curated men's shop C'H'C'M' after his Brooklyn neighborhood, Clinton Hill. When I walked in, he said he'd seen me walking my dog that morning in the 'hood. Thank god I wasn't schlubbing it on the dog walk and was dressed in a similiar style to the modern classics that Sweetu stocks at **C'H'C'M**. If I were a guy, I'd want my wardrobe solely supplied by this place, with styles that could keep me looking good on walks today, tomorrow, and ten years from Thursday. From oxfords to striped shirts, bandanas to the perfect Mackintosh coat—men, you'll get more compliments wearing the clothes from here than the handsomest dog in town.

clic bookstore
& gallery

vintage, new- and limited-edition art and fashion books

255 Centre Street
Corner of Broome (Soho) *map S26*
6: Spring Street
212.966.2766
www.clicbookstore.com

tue - sun noon - 7p
online shopping

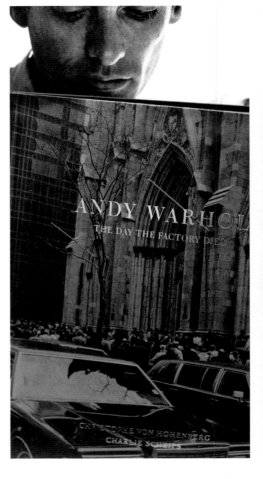

Yes, Please: *books about: guy bourdin, david lachapelle, araki, julie blackmon, matthew rolston, malick sidibe, peter beard, helmut newton*

KW: I used to imagine that I would be a fashion photographer. The closest I got was when I shot my roommate and her friend, styled with layers of pearls and lace gloves à la Madonna in her "Like a Virgin" era. After this fleeting stab at photographic glory, I decided others were better suited for this gig. I didn't lose my love of the craft, though, and have avidly collected photography books ever since—starting with Bruce Weber's *O Rio de Janiero*. **Clic Bookstore** is therefore like photonip to me. If I could, I would transfer the entire store to my own personal library.

creatures of comfort

cool labels, clothing and accessories

205 Mulberry Street
Between Kenmare and Spring
(Nolita) *map S27*
6: Spring Street > N/R: Prince Street
212.925.1005
www.creaturesofcomfort.us

twitter @creaturesnyla
mon - sat 11a - 7p sun noon - 6p
online shopping

Yes. Please: *creatures of comfort collection, ld tuttle pony hair & leather sandal, sylvain le hen hair barrettes, bless x ssm indigo zipper shorts, arts + science black sheer dress*

JO: What a wonderful space to walk into after pushing through the clatter of another Little Italy street fair. Need to get away from the throngs on the street? Or just a new bright colored piece of clothing? Enter **Creatures of Comfort**—an airy, sun-soaked atrium full of clothing bursting with colors, textures and artful retail arrangements that will lift your spirits. There's a men's side, a women's side, and most months, a special capsule exhibit, showcasing things like ceramics from Japan. Ask for Louise if you need a hand—she's sweet and chic and will point out a pair of blue zippered shorts that will really brighten the rest of your day.

extra

fall in love with america again

10 Extra Place
Between First and Second
(Nolita) *map S28*
F: 2nd Ave > 6: Bleecker
212.677.7465
www.extra-nyc.com

mon - thu noon - 7p sat - sun 1 - 7p

Yes, Please: *vintage chevrolet jean jacket, vintage navajo pouches, vintage leica cameras, american folk art, post overalls shirts, post overalls jackets, post overalls chinos*

JO: Extra extra! Japanese Americana rules. This cultural exchange gets a solid high five from historical fashionistas. Two countries once at war have found a mutual love: common-sense workwear designs made newly relevant in these bootstrapping times. **Extra** owner Koji Kusakabe is this movement's unassuming ambassador. Kusakabe devoted himself to vintage while traveling across all 49 states (excepting Alaska). Then his wife said, "You have too much stuff," and found him this secret space. The result? A perfectly curated collection of amazing folk artifacts, and the only spot to carry his friend's line, Post Overalls! I swear, I just wanted to move in.

haus interior

an interior designer's home shop

250 Elizabeth Street
Between Houston and Prince
(Nolita) *mapS29*
F/V: Second Avenue
B/D/F/V: Broadway - Lafayette
212.741.0455
www.hausinterior.com

twitter @hausinterior
mon - sat 11a - 7p sun noon - 6p
online shopping. design services

Yes, Please: *seagrass cubes, fog linen napkins, vintage navy award pillows, brass trophy lamp, brushstroke plate, roost glass canteen*

AB: Television is chock-a-block with the scourge of reality programming, which includes shows featuring every-day people who imagine themselves interior designers. And though these shows make it seem like someone with no experience could miraculously transform into a gifted designer overnight, this is nothing more than good old-fashioned fantasy. If you want the real deal, visit Nina Freudenberger at **Haus Interior**. Not only will you be influenced by her fresh design vision, but you can walk out of here with pieces that work with your bank balance. Good design does come at a price: affordable.

hung ry
hand-pulled, organic chinese noodles
and more

55 Bond Street
Between Lafayette and Bowery
(Nolita) *map E46*
B/D/F/V/M: Broadway - Lafayette
N/R: Prince > 6: Bleecker
212.677.4864
www.hung-ry.com

tue - sun noon - 11p
lunch. dinner
$$ reservations accepted

Yes, Please: *chilled lobster in cucumber broth soup with*
pea shoots & tofu, carrot broth soup with charred kazu &
sesame, hand-pulled noodles made to order

JO: I took my mom to Hung Ry when she was in town. We didn't have a reservation, but they seated us at the bar, no problem. Turns out, these were the best seats in the house. From here we could watch the broad shouldered noodle-master hand pull the star ingredient in all of **Hung Ry**'s delicious soups. He stretches and swings each portion of dough to order, which either means thin or thick, according to your preference. From there Chef Michael and his team take over, putting together organic, seasonal ingredients into soul-satisfying soups. Mom was so impressed, we made sure to tip the noodle-maker.

joanne hendricks, cookbooks...

vintage cookbooks and more

488 Greenwich Street
Between Canal and Spring (Soho) *map S30*
1: Canal Street
212.226.5731
www.joannehendrickscookbooks.com

daily 11:30a - 7p (call before you come)
online shopping

Yes, Please: *bocca series of cookbooks, "the gastronomical me" by m.f.k. fisher, "jane grigson's vegetable book" by jane grigson, vintage menus, swid powell zurich service*

KW: I am married to a really good cook. But he doesn't use cookbooks. He's the master of a little of this, a dash of that—*et voila*, coq au vin! I, on the other hand, am a bit challenged in the culinary arts. When I use his methodology, I get soup cookies. So cookbooks are my friends. Especially vintage ones with beautiful illustrations, and **Joanne Hendricks** has a stunning collection. This tucked-away nook of a bookstore in a federal-style row house is around the corner from the legendary Ear Inn, where you can take your just-bought copy of *Toasts You Ought To Know* to impress your bar mates.

johnson trading gallery
collectible furniture

490 Greenwich Street
Between Canal and Spring (Soho) *map S31*
1: Canal Street
212.925.1110
www.johnsontradinggallery.com

mon - fri 11a - 7p sat noon - 6p
online shopping (first dibs)

Yes, Please: *rafael de cardenas, max lamb, joseph heidecker, ben jones , kwangho lee, aranda/lasch, mario dal fabbro, simon hasan, greg lynn, ricky clifton*

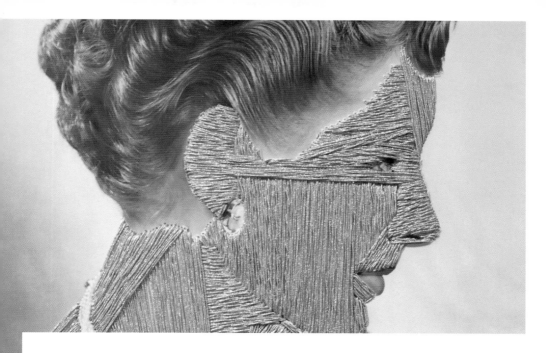

KW: As I was leaving Joanne Hendricks, the October rain kicked into a full downpour and I put my umbrella in horizontal shield position. A couple of doors down I chanced being permanently blinded by rain daggers to take a peek in the window of **Johnson Trading Gallery**. What caught my attention was the Kwangho Lee "knitted" sofa made of black rubber tubing. I needed to see some more, come hell or high water. Inside was what I had been scouring the city for: unusual, artful, collectible, contemporary furniture. If you believe that furnishings can double as artistic statements, **JTG** will delight.

kiosk

eclectic finds from all over the world

95 Spring Street, Second Floor
Between Mercer and Broadway (Soho) *map S32*
R/W: Prince Street > 6: Spring Street
212.226.8601
www.kioskkiosk.com

twitter @kioskkiosk
mon - sat noon - 7p
online shopping

Yes, Please: *horsehair hand broom & red metal dustpan, natural disk rattle, lavender oil from provence, danish dishbrush, red dot tenugui*

AB: NYC has always been a place where retail risk-takers abound. But then came the downturn, and some of these visionaries went by the wayside. So what's left is a number of hardy survivors, and playing it safe seems a reasonable thing to do. So who's still pushing the envelope? **Kiosk**. This always has been and remains a one-of-a-kind retail experience where carefully curated items are culled from Alisa Grifo's adventures abroad. Mini-exhibitions are constantly in rotation. At last check, the Groundhog's Day theme was happening. Need some nut creme from Sweden?

matta

globally inspired clothing, accessories and home décor

241 Lafayette Street
Between Prince and Spring (Nolita) *map S33*
6: Spring Street
212.343.9399
www.mattany.com

daily 11:30a - 7p
online shopping

Yes, Please: *matta: silk & cotton tunics & dresses, dupatta scarf, sarongs, koli sandals, rajasthani blanket, metallic tote bag, dhurri rug*

AB: My friend Anne is one of those women who could wear a paper bag and still look chic. This has to do with her innate sense of style and, most importantly, her way with accessories. When we were wandering around Nolita together, we aimed toward **Matta** and their beautiful ethnic-inspired wares. Anne loves the metallic totes here and I, following my own inner accessorizing voice, was drawn to the tunics and the dupatta scarves with their tasseled ends. After shopping here, even the most accessory-challenged will feel more confident in their ability to wear a paper bag and look great.

meg cohen
design shop
luxe cashmere accessories

59 Thompson Street
Between Spring and Broome
(Soho) *map S34*
C/E: Spring Street
212.966.3733
www.megcohendesign.com

mon - sat 11a - 7p sun 11a - 6p
online shopping

Yes, Please: *meg cohen: scarves, hats, gloves, serapes, cashmere blanket, cotton change purse, men's accessories; vintage cuff links, vintage charm necklaces*

AB: When it comes to keeping warm during the dregs of winter (and this one has been a doozy), style often gets thrown out the window. But my new friend **Meg Cohen** has solved this quandary for me with her gorgeous knits. Before you could say "abominable snowman," I had snapped up a cashmere head scarf and fingerless mittens. There were a number of other treasures and curiosities that appealed and were calling my name, but I decided to ignore the siren's call, knowing that I would be back in spring to stock up for the warm months.

min
new york

niche apothecary and fragrance atelier

117 Crosby Street
Between Prince and Houston
(Soho) *map S35*
N/R Train: Prince
B/D/F/M/6: Broadway - Lafayette
212.206.6366
www.min.com

twitter @minnewyork
tue - sat noon - 8p sun - mon noon - 6p
online shopping. custom orders.
registries. concierge

Yes, Please: *min new york fragrances, santa maria novella, penhaligon's, geo f. trumper, kilian, miller harris, l'artisan parfumeur, amouage, temps des reves, kent*

JO: With its dark wood interior, black leather Chesterfield couch and gunmetal chests brimming with goodies, this apothecary and atelier for men's and women's grooming will satisfy a real nose, but won't intimidate a novice in the scent world either. MiN New York lets you explore on your own accord. Owner Chad Murawczyk is on hand if you need some advice or some direction, but no rush. He rotates 300 or so fragrances at any given time, with lines from fantastic locales around the world like Côté Bastide, France and Madrid, Spain. Why smell like a NYC cabbie or vestiges of the R train when you can smell like **MiN**?

no. 6 store

*contemporary and vintage
women's clothing*

6 Centre Market Place
Between Broome and Grand
(Little Italy) *map S36*
6: Spring Street
212.226.5759
www.no6store.com

mon - sat noon - 7p sun noon - 6p

Yes. Please: *no. 6: light woodland floral silk print dress,
black velvet & lace overlap dress, leather buckle clog boot;
aesa jewelry, wendy nichol bags*

AB: The first time I visited No. 6, I felt like I was walking into a party of good friends at someone's house. Ladies were lounging on the couch giving advice to each other while trying on various pieces. One of the owners was pulling clothing like she was grabbing items from her own closet. I could have felt like an outsider intruding, but the exact opposite was true. The vibe here is nothing but warm and friendly, which makes you want to sit down and pull on a pair of **No. 6**'s of-the-moment clog boots or slip into one of the sweet vintage-inspired dresses. If you still find me here next month, don't be surprised.

ochre store
rustic modern housewares

462 Broome Street
Between Mercer and Greene (Soho) *map S37*
6: Spring Street
212.414.4332
www.ochrestore.com
www.canvashomestore.com

mon - sat 11a - 7p sun noon - 6p
online shopping

Yes, Please: *ochre: canvas furniture collection, collective 462, vintage pieces, organic linens; papuro journels, chemex glass coffee maker*

AB: Usually I like a place based on the visual aspects. But at **Ochre**, my initial love feelings came from how it smelled. Not that I've been in a country farmhouse slash urbane Argentine mountain home, but I think that's how it would smell. As for the visuals, they are just as good here: striking furniture and minimalistic accessories like wooden planks and handwoven organic linen napkins. It's so calming here, which is such a contrast to the world of traffic and steel just outside the doors. Take a scan of **Ochre**'s world and know that a piece of it can be in your world also.

palmer trading company

northeastern man essentials

137 Sullivan Street
Between Prince and Houston
(Soho) *map S38*
C/E: Spring Street
646.360.4557
www.palmertrading.com

daily noon - 8p
online shopping. custom orders / design
design services

Yes. Please: *palmer trading co. shirts, made in brooklyn, palmer trading co. chinos (made in mass), oak street boot makers (made in maine), brimfield duffle bag, man candles*

JO: Men get the best shops. No offense to the wonderful women's shops in this town, but I'd like to be a man (just for a day or two) just to shop at **Palmer Trading Co.**, a store hand-built by owners Willy and David. I'd be a normal bloke, manly enough to swing an axe and split logs for a nice fireside chat with my pals Hemingway and Whitman. At some point, Ernest would ask me where he could get a shirt as great as mine. With a special front pocket for his pen, made in the small mill town of Fall River, Mass., a **PTC** would look great on Ernie.

partners & spade
art gallery and playground of creativity

BACKDATED CONFIDENCE TROPHIES

40 Great Jones Street
Between Bowery and Lafayette
(Nolita) *map S39*
6: Bleecker Street
646.861.2827
www.partnersandspade.com

sat noon - 7p sun noon - 6p
mon - fri by appointment only
online shopping

ETCH-A-SKETCH
IN THE SKY

Yes, Please: *partner & spade books, handmade arrows, assorted succulents & cacti, backdated confidence trophies, drawer full of vintage smut*

JO: Do you have a sense of humor? No? Then come to **Partners & Spade** and you could buy or borrow one. There's a cheeky wit among all the offerings and artistic displays in this gallery slash fun room slash one-of-a-kind items place. You'll find things like a carved monkey covered with a band-aid (monkey pimple?) or a boxed self-help set. Only two creative men with great taste and generous spirits named Anthony Sperduti and Andy Spade could give birth to this kind of retail concept and share the experience with us. Thanks to them for the gift of humor.

saturdays
surf nyc
surf shop / coffee shop / backyard paradise

31 Crosby Street
Between Broome and Grand
(Soho) *map S40*
4/6: Spring Street > N/R: Canal Street
212.966.7875
www.saturdaysnyc.com

twitter @saturdaysnyc
mon - fri 8:30a - 7p sat - sun 10a - 7p
online shopping

Yes, Please: *saturdays surf nyc: printed tees, x porter tote bag, enis board short; hoplite wet suit, gato heroi surfboards, baxter atlantic beach soap*

JO: I am not a surfer, but I am a pro backyard-patio-coffee-drinker. Luckily **Saturdays Surf Shop** happily entertains both surf-and-shore creatures. This is a place where I can take my out-of-town guests and they can talk to manager Angus, discover that they know the same surfer in Perth, Australia and buy new board shorts. While they do this, I'll sneak out to the cool back patio with a lovely latte made at the in-store coffee bar and read one of **Saturdays'** many satisfying publications in the sun. Spending time here is like taking a mini-break.

sunrise mart

japanese specialty market

494 Broome Street
Between Wooster and Broadway
(Soho) *map E47*
C/E: Spring Street
212.219.0033

daily 10a - 10p
light meals. grocery
$-$$ first come, first served

Yes, Please: *pocari sweat drink, green tea with brown rice, otokomae tofu, sticky rice, pink salt, udon noodles, extensive rice varities*

AB: I've come up with a new diet—The Japanese Candy diet. I want to clarify immediately that this concept is slightly different from the idea of hara hachi bunme, which is eating until you are about 80 percent full. My Japanese Candy diet is based off of a daily intake of the types of treats that one can find at **Sunrise Mart**: Pucca chocolate, Yim-Yam, yuzu gummies, milk candies—and it is imperative to make yourself gloriously, 100% full. This will then create a healthy glow of sugar satisfaction. If you don't believe in the brilliance of my diet, you can also grab a bento box here or a multitude of Asian groceries.

the smile

rustic meet / greet / eat café

26 Bond Street
Between Lafayette and Bowery
(Nolita) *map E48*
B/D/F/V/M: Broadway - Lafayette
6: Bleecker
646.329.5836
www.thesmilenyc.com

twitter @thesmilenyc
mon - fri 8a - midnight
sat - sun 10a - midnight
breakfast. lunch. dinner. brunch
$-$$ reservations accepted

Yes. Please: *cappuccino, chocolate & brie baguette, smoked salmon & lemon caper cream cheese sandwich, harissa honey roasted chicken sandwich, roasted leg of lamb*

JO: The atmosphere at The Smile makes you feel creative. Here you'll eat with writers, art directors, photographers, gallery assistants, and other casually stylish, hyphenated talents. These people could lackadaisically be plotting to take over the world or just enjoying a catch up lunch with old friends. I've done both. Rather than the "power lunch" of old, where your social standing depends on which power table you're seated at, here at **The Smile**, everyone is too busy enjoying themselves and eating well to bother with egos. Order a sammie served with addictive North Fork chips and keep talking shop 'til dinner time. It's less regimented, but way more fun.

wendy nichol

gorgeous leather goods and jewelry

147 Sullivan Street
Between Prince and Houston
(Soho) *map S41*
C/E: Spring Street
212.431.4171
www.wendynicholnyc.com

twitter @wendynicholnyc
sat - wed noon - 7p thu - fri noon - 8p
online shopping. custom orders / design

Yes, Please: *wendy nichol: gold small dt pyramid hoops, gold mix & match studs, black canyon duffle bag, leather & pony pouches, fez weave bullet bag*

JO: Wendy Nichol works out of her Soho store, along with a number of industrious assistants. I admire this old tradition of apprenticeship—it's a great way to learn by doing. Getting to peer into Wendy and her team's creative process lets you get a feel for the craftsmanship that goes into the pieces for sale—like the hand-braided leather details on drawstring aztec bullet bags. Seeing the work happen right before your eyes can't help but make your purchase that much more special. You'll have a story to go along with your handcrafted carryall—a piece that will get better with age, just like you.

manhattan

east village

eat

shop

abraço

*espresso counter with exceptional
small plates*

**86 East Seventh Street
Between First and Second
(East Village)** *map E 49*
**4/6: Astor Place > L: 1st Avenue
R/W: Eighth Street
www.abraconyc.com**

tue - sat 8a - 4p sun 9a - 4p
coffee / tea. lunch. treats
$ cash only. first come, first served

Yes, Please: *individually dripped coffee, café cortado,
roasted vegetable with cheddar fritatta, sunchoke ricotta
& mint sandwich, olive oil cake, pistachio cookie*

JFD: With a hearty, "What you need, brotha?" Jamie, the magnetic owner and coffee puller of **Abraço**, greets his customers. Chances are, if you go to this small espresso counter, you are seriously in need of one of Jamie's skillfully made, perfectly balanced coffee drinks. What you might not have realized, until you bite into one, is that you also need chef/partner Elizabeth's dense, flavor-rich olive oil cake. And now, I'm telling you, brothas and sistas, that what you really, really need is to check in here daily. Once will do, but twice is better.

change of season

hand-picked past-season gems

341 East Ninth Street
Between First and Second
(East Village) *map S42*
L: First Avenue > 6: Astor Place
212.420.7770
www.changeofseasonnyc.com

twitter @cosboutiquenyc
tue - sun 1 - 7:30p
online shopping

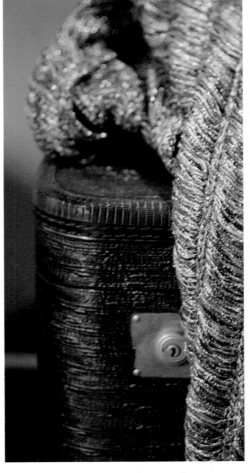

Yes, Please: *vivienne westwood, commes des garçons, see by chloe, balenciaga, galliano, coming soon by yohji yamamoto, viktor & rolf, dries van noten*

JFD: "Out with the old and in with the new" works perfectly well if you have an inexhaustible budget and you're obsessed with having the flavor-of-this-precise-moment item. If there's a steep discount, however, might you amend it to "in with the almost new"? That's the modus operandi behind **Change of Season**, whose owners skip overseas to get designer label pieces and fly them back here to sell at great prices in the "off-season." In my world there is no off-season, so velvet blazer by Coming Soon, you best believe I plan to be claiming you soon.

dirt candy

extravagant vegetarian fare

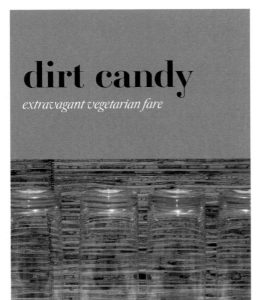

430 East Ninth Sreet
Between First and A (East Village) *map E50*
L: First Avenue > 6: Astor Place
212.228.7732
www.dirtcandynyc.com

twitter @dirtcandy
tue - wed 5:30 - 10p
thu - sat 5:30 - 10:30p
dinner. beer / wine
$$ reservations recommended

Yes, Please: *o8 michel torino don david torrontes reserve, jalapeño hush puppies with maple butter, kimchi donuts, asparagus paella, golden beet pappardelle*

JFD: I admit, like many conscious eaters of this era, I'm sometimes a bit tortured by my feelings about meat. I can go on about this at length, but "boorrrriiinngg," I hear Amanda Cohen, the owner/chef of **Dirt Candy**, interrupt in my head. She'll tell you, in her tartly hilarious blog, that she's not interested in your health or your politics. What she enjoys are vegetables, and she has found some innovative ways to cook them. And while a few of the dishes bear the sometimes perverse (and entertaining) hallmarks of molecular gastronomy, others are simply prepared vegetables that just taste really good.

double crown

the flavors of the british empire
in southeast asia

316 Bowery
Corner of Bleecker (East Village) *map E51*
6: Bleecker Street
212.254.0350
www.doublecrown-nyc.com

twitter @double_crown
see website for hours
lunch. dinner. brunch. afternoon tea
$$ reservations recommended

Yes. Please: *strawberry & basil boozy tea, sweet
lemongrass tea; devonshire tea: coconut labne, piccalilli,
coronation chicken scone*

KW: During a typical NYC weekend, the streets of the city are flooded with locals, bridge and tunnelers, and tourists. To walk on Broadway in Soho requires a stealth ability to dodge the masses armed with their bulging shopping bags. Suggestions for a calmer weekend experience? Head east for afternoon tea at **Double Crown**. This lushly designed ode to British colonialism in India and Singapore is the perfect spot to settle in (and is great for lunch and dinner also). The tea set is piled high, and the tea—if you so choose—can be boozy. And when the night comes and you're in the mood for more of a bar scene, head through the concealed doorway to **Madam Geneva** to continue the relaxation.

john derian company

glorious decoupage and more

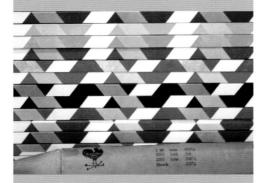

6 East Second Street
Between Bowery and Second
(East Village) *map S43*
F/V: Second Avenue
212.677.3917
www.johnderian.com

tue - sun noon - 7p

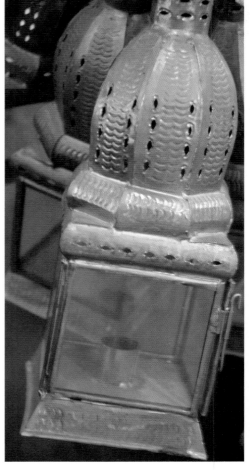

Yes, Please: *john derian: decoupage plates & platters,*
paperweights; astier de villatte collaboration, artemas
quibble leather bracelets, hugo guiness prints, feather dusters

AB: John Derian might be well on his way to taking over the world, which I personally think would be pretty great. I am constantly coming across his decoupage designs in stores across the country. I can almost always guarantee the place is good if **John Derian** is sold at an establishment. Nothing, though, compares to the experience of John's own store, which is a world of wonderful and beyond. If you haven't been here before, you are missing out on an extraordinary retail experience. It's one of my favorite places in this city.

mayahuel

abundant, high quality tequila and delicious mexican fare

304 East Sixth Street
Between First and Second
(East Village) *map E52*
6: Astor Place
212.253.5888
www.mayahuelny.com

twitter @mayahuelny
mon - sat 6p - 2a sun 2p - midnight
dinner. brunch. full bar
$$-$$$ first come, first served

Yes, Please: *dozens of tequilas & mezcals, beer cocktails, popcorn with lime, cotija cheese & ancho chili, mole braised chicken tamales, hanger steak over summer corn pudding*

JFD: To be aged and rested sounds alright to me. You'll find these two categories of sipping tequila—"anejo" and "reposado"—at **Mayahuel**, along with dozens of younger, rarer and somewhat exotic relatives of the Mexican liquor. Obviously this is a place for agave enthusiasts. The rest of us, who don't exactly qualify as enthusiasts, who identify more as "never drinking tequila again until I can restore my dignity following those 36 lost hours in Phoenix and/or until I find that rental car" might be excited about the seriously delicious Mexican food here and a nice beer or two.

northern spy food co.

local and regional good stuff

511 East 12th Street
Between A and B (East Village) *map E53*
L: First Avenue > F/V: Second Avenue
212.228.5100
www.northernspyfoodco.com

twitter @northernspyfood
see website for hours
breakfast. lunch. dinner. brunch. grocery.
wine / beer
$$ first come, first served

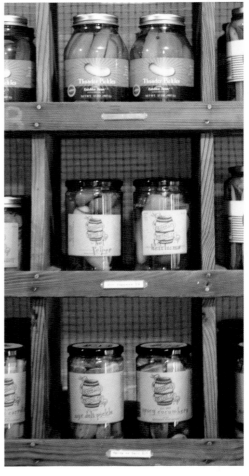

Yes, Please: *quince seltzer, blue point oatmeal stout, red bean puree, pork terrine, squid & mussels, roasted chicken, stewed runner beans*

JFD: Back when I lived in Brooklyn, a sign appeared one day on a neighboring building announcing "The Vermont Store." I got really excited, imagining the fresh maple syrup and delicious cheeses I'd have access to. Instead, the guy sold hairspray, Christmas trees and maps. Major letdown. What I wanted is what **Northern Spy** is: a provisioner that makes and sells only small batch and artisanal foods from New York and New England. Honeys, syrups, pickles, milk, cheese, jams—all the good stuff. And there's a restaurant, too. It's all here in this little rural part of the East Village.

obscura
antiques &
oddities

fun, weird things

280 East Tenth Street
Between First and A (East Village) *map S44*
L: First Avenue > 6: Astor Place
212.505.9251
www.obscuraantiques.com

twitter @obscuraantiques
mon - sun noon - 8p

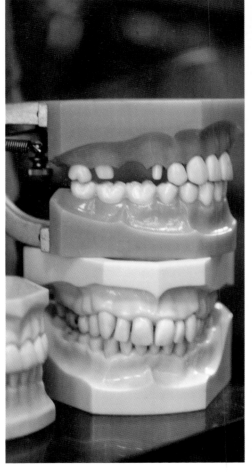

Yes, Please: *victorian taxidermy, medical oddities, freemason paraphernalia, masks, vintage photos & postcards, capes, apothecary products*

JFD: How's this for a cross-section of society? When I asked **Obscura Antique**'s owner Mike what kind of customer regularly frequents his store, he offered: movie people, fetishists and corporate types (with Jon Peters, you get three in one). Movie types I can see: props are needed when filming flicks like *Seven* or *Saw*. Fetishists: the masks, capes and medical oddities compute. Corporate types: I'm assuming that folks like myself fall into this category, as I enjoyed scanning the shelves for antique false teeth and pickled lobster embryos. My take: The items here may be obscura, but they're also fun-a.

porchetta

slow-cooked italian fast food

110 East Seventh Street
Between First and A (East Village) *map E54*
6: Astor Place > F/V: Second Avenue
212.777.2151
www.porchettanyc.com

twitter @porchettanyc
sun - thu 11:30a - 10p fri - sat 11:30a - 11p
lunch. dinner
$-$$ first come, first served

Yes, Please: *lemonade, boylston sodas, porchetta sandwich, slow-cooked pork ragu with grilled ciabatta, pumpkin soup, chicory salad with garlic dressing, biscotti*

JFD: In Italy, porchetta is hawked out of white vans, which the locals, if they have any sense, chase down the street like kids pursuing a Mr. Softee truck. Just reading about porchetta gets me salivating. In three Wikipedia sentences, these words appear: "savory, fatty, moist, deboned, meat, fat, crispy skin, rolled, spitted, roasted over wood, heavily salted, stuffed, garlic, rosemary, fennel, wild herbs." I swear I'm not too lazy to write my own blurb; I just don't think I could improve on that. Better than reading is going to the tiny **Porchetta**, where chef Sara's pork is *molto bene*. And since some think there is life beyond pork, visit Sara's new spot, **Porsena**, where pasta is the order of the day.

stock vintage

early american menswear

143 East 13th Street
Between Third and Fourth
(East Village) *map S45*
L: Third Avenue
4/5/6: 14th Street-Union Square
212.505.2505

mon - fri noon - 8p sat noon - 7p
sun noon - 6p

Yes, Please: *early american men's vintage: boots, denim, shirting, leather jackets, fedoras, sweaters, overalls*

JFD: When I walked into Stock Vintage, there was a big military duffel bag overturned with tangled mounds of sweaters spilling out of it and greedy customers sifting through it like a bunch of 1849ers panning for gold. I guess you could say that the vintage clothing here is a kind of gold, because it's harder than heck to find. Owner Melissa Howard scours the country to bring back dungarees and work boots and the like to this cabin-like shop. While I don't know where she mines, I imagine her digging through Nebraskan attics and Iowan closets to find this well-worn clothing that still has decades left of wear.

the beagle

classic drink / food pairings

162 Avenue A
Between 10th and 11th
(East Village) *map E55*
L Train: 1st Avenue > 6 Train: Astor Place
212.228.6900
www.thebeaglenyc.com

tue - wed, sun 6p - 1a thu - sat 6p - 2a
dinner. full bar
$$ reservations accepted

Yes, Please: *preakness cocktail, roasted lamb neck & rye pairing board, burrata & gin pairing board, golden beets with greek yogurt & marcona almonds, sherry cobbler*

JO: A friend of mine has two beagles, and even in their youth these sausages-on-legs carried themselves like they'd been around forever. Similarly, though only three weeks old on my visit, **The Beagle** felt like a classic East Village establishment. Owner Matt has enough restaurant cred (he co-owns Portland, Oregon's **Clyde Common**) to know what counts—attention to detail. Like the white/blue-striped cotton straws that cheer up the fantastic cocktails. Speaking of drinks, the bartender Dan let me behind the bar to see his chemistry set—tumblers of fresh-squeezed citrus and little tinctures of this and that. When the shaking is over and the viscose liquor is poured, **The Beagle** pairs its drinks with the kind of food that soaks up a cocktail perfectly.

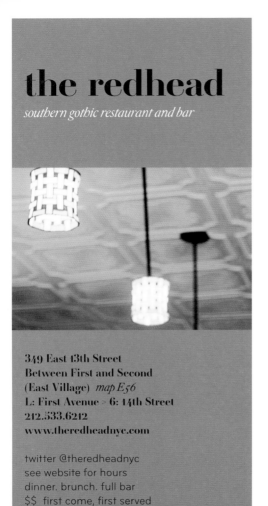

the redhead

southern gothic restaurant and bar

349 East 13th Street
Between First and Second
(East Village) *map E56*
L: First Avenue > 6: 14th Street
212.533.6242
www.theredheadnyc.com

twitter @theredheadnyc
see website for hours
dinner. brunch. full bar
$$ first come, first served

Yes, Please: *ommegang rare vos, sazerac, soft pretzel with kentucky beer cheese, one-eyed caesar salad, creamy parsnip soup with poached lobster, buttermilk fried chicken*

JFD: You'd think that the promise of bacon peanut brittle would be what lured me to The Redhead. Good guess, but wrong. What first enticed me was learning that this restaurant had originally opened as a bar, became a fixture in the 'hood, and then gently transitioned into a fine, southern-inflected restaurant, home to some killer crispy buttermilk chicken. So, it was the "bar done good" story that got me in the door. Then a series of bayou-inspired dishes rooted me to my seat. And the chocolate car bomb at dinner's end—that just dropped me to the floor.

manhattan

lower east side, chinatown

eat

shop

assembly
new york

just about perfect
men's and women's boutique

170 Ludlow Street
Between Houston and Stanton
(Lower East Side) *map S46*
F/V: Second Avenue
212.253.5393
www.assemblynewyork.com

daily noon - 9p
online shopping. custom order

Yes, Please: *assembly collection, 69, alexander yamaguchi, a detacher, arielle de pinto, boessert/schorn, christophe lemaire, anve, lgr sunglasses, d.co*

KW: This is a town where you need to affect a certain level of blasé. Acting overly enthusiastic might get you banned to the outer boroughs or sent packing on the first flight to happy bubbly land. I've had many years to practice this disconnected nonchalance and can bring it with the best of them. But often I don't care if I'm being cool, and I actually—gasp—show that I like something or someplace. For example, **Assembly New York**. I liked just about every damn piece of extremely wearable yet super modern clothing here and had no problems saying so. In fact, I liked a pair of boots here so much they are now mine.

classic
coffee shop

a slice of the real new york city

56 Hester Street
Corner of Ludlow (Chinatown) *map E57*
F: East Broadway
917.685.3306

wed - mon 7a - 8:30p
breakfast. lunch
$ first come, first served

Yes, Please: *classic egg cream, little hug juice, egg sandwich on a roll, grilled cheese sandwich, sardines sandwich, ruffles, wrigley's gum*

KW: If you are going to spend any time in this city, there are certain food items that are imperative to the NYC experience. A bubbling hot slice of white pizza. A skyscraper of a pastrami sandwich. And the breakfast of choice for hordes of on-the-run New Yorkers: an egg sandwich. There are a number of ways to order this, but my favorite is a mini omelette tucked inside a buttered roll. Add a dash of salt and pepper. Devour. If you are downtown, grab one at **Classic Coffee Shop**. This tiny neighborhood diner is a slice of old New York, which makes it a breath of fresh air.

dear :
rivington+

wearable avant garde and curated pieces
for home

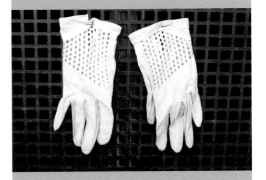

95 Rivington Street
Between Ludlow and Orchard
(Lower East Side) *map S47*
F/J/M/Z: Essex Street - Delancey
212.673.3494
www.dearrivington.com

daily noon - 8p
custom orders / design

Yes, Please: *dear: clothing, shoes & accessories;*
vintage: martin margiela, yohji yamamoto, issey miyake,
upstairs dedicated to vintage furniture

KW: I worked in retail in NYC during in the '80s. My first gig was at Kansai Yamamoto, where I sold cartoonish asymmetrical, appliquéd sweaters and cartoonesque designs. Then I worked at Charivari Workshop and most all my dosh was spent on acquiring Comme des Garçons, Yohji Yamamoto and Matsuda pieces. I admit, I still have a soft spot for that early era of Japanese clothing design, and I felt its essence in full force at **Dear : Rivington+**. Yes ladies, you can wear a parachute pant if it's designed by Heyja. And if you lust after the original pieces, the stock of vintage Japanese design here is excellent.

fenton fallon

'80s fabulous jewelry and vintage clothing

(Lower East Side) *map S48*
www.danalorenz.com

twitter @fentonfallon
online shopping

Yes, Please: *all points west lasso cuff, wild at heart earrings, boffs bracelet, cairo chandelier earrings, infinity segmented necklace, isis cuff, labyrinth maze knot ring*

KW: Without doing a lick of research, I'm going to take a stab in the dark and guess that Dana Lorenz named her jewelry line after Fallon Carrington, the naughty minx on *Dynasty*. And Fenton? Maybe he was the butler on the show. But let's get back to the 21st century and the real story. Dana's first line was **Fenton**, which is very Alexis Carrington in both price and style. Next came **Fallon**, which, like its imagined namesake, is younger and sassier and has a lighter price tag. The two lines used to commingle at a space the size of Krystle Carrington's boudoir on Freeman's Alley, but rumor has it Dana is looking for a larger location. So for now you'll have to buy these bold '80s style pieces off her website.

gesamtkunstwerk
year-round flea market designer showcase

9 Clinton Street
Between Houston and Stanton
(Lower East Side) *map S 49*
J/M/Z: Essex > F Train: Delancey
646.476.9100
www.cantspellit.com

twitter @gkwerk
tue - sun noon - 8p
custom orders / design

Yes, Please: *verameat double rings, charlene foster pyrex glass chain necklace, accessories by ash knot rope necklace, zeichen press greeting cards, mauro baiocco painting*

JO: This shop's name, Gesamtkunstwerk, is virtually unpronounceable, but thankfully the store is very approachable. It was started by Allie and Lucia, two Cooper Union grads who met in school and decided to bring together their fellow "thing-makers" under one roof. **Werk**, as its easier to call, is like an all-weather flea market where no matter the season and weather—rain, sleet, snow or shine—you can find thoughtfully designed and crafted jewelry, small-press stationery, art and toys. Just the kind of NYC souvenirs to prove you came, saw and shopped local.

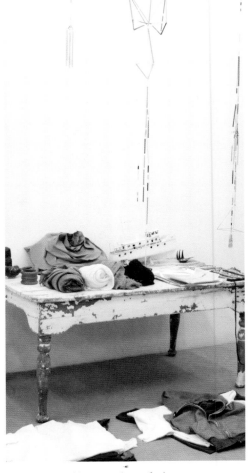

maryam nassir zadeh

retail storytelling

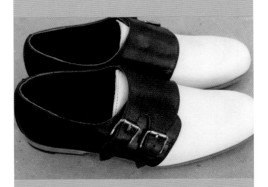

123 Norfolk Street
Corner of Rivington
(Lower East Side) *map S50*
F/J/M/Z: Essex Street - Delancey
212.673.6405
www.maryamnassirzadeh.com

daily noon - 8p

Yes, Please: *golden goose, electric feathers, carven, veronique leroy, eatable of many orders, all for the mountain, dieppa restrepo, jasmin shokrian*

KW: Though I want to believe I'm a good storyteller, deep down I know that's a pipe dream. When I tell a story I take forever to get to the interesting part, and the poor people listening get stuck hearing a litany of "umm"s and "like"s. Yawn. **Maryam Nassir Zadeh** is a great storyteller, and she doesn't have to utter a word. To hear her tales, all you need to do is walk in the door of her eponymous retail world. Walking through here is like turning the pages of a Gabriel Garcia Marquez novel. Each vignette of beautifully sourced clothing and accessories is positioned to make you ponder, and then acquire.

mei li wah bakery

old school chinese pork bun masters

64 Bayard Street
Between Elizabeth and Mott
(Chinatown) *map E58*
J/N/Q/Z: Canal Street
212.966.7866

daily 7a - 10:30p
breakfast. lunch. light meals.
coffee / tea. treats
$ first come, first served

Yes, Please: *milky coffee or tea, shrimp rice noodle rolls, baked pork buns, steamed pork buns, pineapple buns*

JO: The first time my parents took me and my brother as kids for dim sum in a scantily decorated, poorly lit room with tin "silverware," it was a revelation—we hit the roof with delight. A family favorite at dim sum joints are the shrimp rice rolls. The simple combination of shrimp, sauce and noodle is incredibly satisfying. **Mei Li Wah** does them justice, but the pork buns are the stars here. The baked bun is golden and flaky and my pick for the best in Chinatown. Plus, nothing beats the aroma of freshly baked bread wafting in spirals to meet your welcoming nose. Sweet or savory, these buns hit the spot.

moscot

nyc eyewear institution

SOL MOSCOT

GLASSES MADE
WHILE YOU WAIT

118 Orchard Street
Corner of Delancey
(Lower East Side) *map S51*
F: Delancey > B/D: Grand Street J/M/Z:
Essex Street
212.477.3796
www.moscot.com

twitter @moscot
mon - fri 10a - 7p sat 10a - 6p
sun 11a - 6p
online shopping. eye exams

Yes, Please: *moscot originals: the hyman, the nebb, the lemtosh, the miltzen, the yukel; moscot collaboration: the terry le; moscot sun: the grover, the fionah*

JO: If an alien landed on Delancey and asked me what makes NYC so cool, I'd link arms and walk him over to **Moscot.** This eyeglass institution would give me the chance to a) teach the alien about the history of New York's original immigrant class, b) see the who's who of New York creatives wearing their trademark Moscots (Woody Allen, Terry Richardson) and c) debunk the myth that New Yorkers are unfriendly (everyone at **Moscot** helps everyone). Then I'd buy my new extraterrestrial buddy the Lemtosh style glasses (aliens don't carry cash), whereupon he'd look better and be smarter than all the other aliens back home. We'd have a blast.

no. 8b
the brother to project no. 8

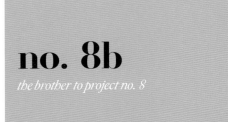

38 Orchard Street
Corner of Hester (Lower East Side) *map S52*
F: East Broadway
212.925.5599
www.projectno8.com

twitter @projectno8
tue - sun noon - 7p

Yes, Please: *various projects suiting, shirting, outerwear & accessories; project no. 8 travel store at the ace hotel, e15 furniture, aspesi coats, hope field boots*

JH: Every time I think about Project No. 8, I wonder what projects numbers 1-7 were. Was project number 1 an eBay shop selling kitten mugs? Maybe project number 2 was hand-painting tea towels. Whatever the earlier projects, what matters is that Brian and Elizabeth opened **Project No. 8**, a seminal retail experience for women. Thankfully they like new projects and recently opened **No. 8b** a few blocks away. It has the same minimalist aesthetic, but **8b** is just for menfolk. Which makes me wonder: was project number 1b selling dog mugs on eBay?

occulter

one-of-a-kind jewelry and memento mori

83.5 Orchard Street
Between Broome and Grand
(Lower East Side) *map S53*
J/M/Z: Essex > F: Delancey
B/D Train: Grand
917.769.2220
www.occulter.org

twitter @occulter001
thu - sun noon - 7p and by appointment
online shopping. custom orders / design

Yes, Please: *occulter black books rubber-sealed paperbacks, occulter black smoke tea, una horse hair bracelet, silver jaw fossil ashtray, salvaged antique piano key breastplate*

JO: You say "Carl Sagan," I say "Cosmos!" This was the first sign that jewelry designer/shop owner Derrick Cruz was a cool-nerd. (Hint: Sagan's show, *Cosmos*, inspired the name **Occulter**.) Cool-nerds take their former nerd tendencies and transform them into art, like Derrick has done here. **Occulter** is the tiniest slice of a shop, literally 150 sq. feet, displaying Derrick's mystical jewelry line, Black Sheep & Prodigal Sons, and a rotating art gallery, which is an expression of modern wonderment. The shop showcases pieces imagined by a stellar creative mind—like a necklace made with a honeycomb dipped in gold and a breastplate made of salvaged ivory piano keys. You'll stare at the craftwerk and stay for the conversation.

reed space

streetwear emporium and sociable art gallery

151 Orchard Street
Between Rivington and Stanton
(Lower East Side) *map S54*
F: 2nd Ave > J/M/Z: Delancey
212.253.0588
www.thereedspace.com

twitter @reedspace
mon - fri 1 - 7p sat - sun noon - 7p
online shopping

Yes, Please: *staple pigeon tees & caps, head porter accessories, stpl design label rain jacket, reed pages (in-house magazine), medicom fabrick x unkle, kid robot staple pigeon*

MI: Reed Space is a more than just a streetwear destination. Yes, discerning dressers who take their sneakers and t-shirts very seriously come here to buy carefully chosen streetwear, shoes, and accessories. But there's also books, gadgets, music, and even a properly hip lip balm. Owner Jeff Staple also uses this LES venue to showcase fine art from his creative friends and limited-run product collaborations that his firm Staple Design creates with everyone from Timbaland to G-Shock. In 2005, fans famously slept outside the store for days just to get their hands on the Staple x Nike SB Pigeon Dunk sneakers. Like I said, **Reed Space** is more than just a destination—it's a bit of a legend.

szeki

jewelry, accessories and apparel

157 Rivington Street
Between Clinton and Suffolk
(Lower East Side) *map S55*
F/J/M/Z: Essex - Delancey
646.243.1789
www.szekinyc.com

mon - sat 11a - 7:30p sun 11a - 7p
online shopping

Yes, Please: *initial necklace, letter charms necklaces, the knot ring, the melted ring, paired earrings, brass bangles, artwood bags, 7115 bags & shoes*

KW: Often when people think about this city, they think BIG. Big buildings, big restaurants and department stores, big crowds, big noise. When I think about this city, I think small. It's all about the nooks and crannies for me. And a notable little store is **Szeki**. Though not so big in size, this place and its owner of the same name have a big heart. Here you can find not only Szeki's charmingly simple jewelry, but also wares ranging from her mom's bag line to one-off pieces she brings in from Asia. Small is good.

the fat radish

seasonal british farm-to-table fare

**17 Orchard Street
Between Hester and Canal
(Lower East Side)** *map E59*
**F: East Broadway
212.300.4053
www.thefatradishnyc.com**

twitter @thefatradish
see website for hours
lunch. dinner. brunch. full bar. grocery
$$ reservations accepted

Yes, Please: *baby beet salad with chamomile & pine nut dressing, sweet pea summer pot pie, colorado lamb with market spinach & hen of the woods mushrooms*

JO: Happy friends make happy food. This is at the heart of **The Fat Radish**. At pre-opeing, I witnessed Nicholas, the chef, prep his stunningly colorful market-fresh food as ebullient manager Steven and the staff arranged the room's rustic decor. All the while jokes flew fast and everyone was smiling. My bet is a smile will appear on your face also once you step inside **The Fat Radish**. David Brooks, *New York Times* columnist, cites a study that concludes this: to improve your happiness, you oughta have dinner with others. These scientists must have eaten here. In fact, I could take my nemesis (Bradley Cooper), my ex, and an angry despot (rhymes with Schmalin), and we'd dine in complete harmony. It's that good!

the ten bells

natural wines, oysters and small plates

247 Broome Street
Between Orchard and Ludlow
(Lower East Side) *map E60*
F/M/Z: Essex - Delancey
212.228.4450
www.thetenbells.com

mon - fri 5p - 2a sat - sun 3p - 2a
dinner. beer / wine
$$ cash only. first come, first served

Yes, Please: *06 arbois pupillin melon, 08 wurtz "cuvee 10 bells" riesling, malpeque oysters, papas bravas, potato & octopus salad, boquerones, hand-cut tartare, chocolate cigars*

JH: I love wine; I just hate talking about it. I would rather drink beer than have to discuss the "chewiness" of a Cabernet Franc. I find that level of fanaticism comparable to a Dungeons and Dragons obsession. This is why I love **The Ten Bells**. Not only are the wines excellent (they only serve natural wines), the atmosphere is like a lively bistro rather than a room filled with gamers dourly discussing wizard-leveling guides. And the staff, though incredibly knowledgeable, don't seem to take themselves too seriously, because they've got better things to do, like shuck me a dozen of those delicious oysters.

vanessa's dumpling house

delicious little dumplings made by talented little hands

118A Eldridge Street
Between Grand and Broome
(Lower East Side) *map E61*
B/D: Grand Street
212.625.8008

mon - sat 7:30a - 10:30p sun 7:30a - 10p
lunch. dinner. treats
$ first come, first served

Yes, Please: *honeydew milk tea, date honey, sesame pancake with egg sandwich, cabbage & pork fried dumplings, pork fried buns, fish ball noodle soup, sour & spicy cucumber*

JH: Supposedly New York is one of the most expensive cities in the world. And yes, my jaw has dropped at the sight of some of my restaurant tabs. But even frugal *moi* can't understand how it's possible to have such an awesome meal at **Vanessa's Dumpling House** for such a low price. Is Vanessa a secret millionaire who makes dumplings for pure pleasure, not monetary gain? If I'm right, it's all the more reason to thank her for some of the best, most inspired dumplings in this city. And don't forget to have the sesame pancake sandwich, which is akin to a chewy Asian panino and, did I mention, cheap?!

victor osborne

downtown milliner

160 Orchard Street
Between Stanton and Rivington
(Lower East Side) *map S56*
F/J/M/Z: Essex - Delancey
212.677.6254
www.victorosborne.com

tue - sun noon - 7p
online shopping. custom orders / design

Yes, Please: *victor osborne: brigitte beret, buckle miles, ester, cloche, diamond cap, stewardess cocktail, trilby, sidecar, marlene, bianca, bowler*

KW: Here's what makes me sad. The end of *Driving Miss Daisy.* "Your Song" by Elton John. And how flat my hair gets when I wear hats. The latter gets me the most, especially when I'm at a place like **Victor Osborne**. These aren't just some random molded felt floozies, but hand-blocked beauties each lovingly created by Victor sitting in the back of his darkly compelling atelier. As I took them all in, I was having visions of a much-needed hair transplant, or maybe just a good old-fashioned perm. Actually, these lids are so great I'll just plan on never taking my chosen one off.

xi'an famous foods

unique middle eastern chinese street food

67 Bayard Street
Between Elizabeth and Mott
(Chinatown) *map E2*
J/N/Q/Z: Canal Street
See website for other locations
www.xianfoods.com

twitter @xianfoods
daily 11a - 9p
lunch. dinner. light meals.
$ cash only. first come, first served

Yes. Please: *liang pi cold skin noodles, spicy cumin lamb burger, stewed oxtail hand-ripped noodles, spicy & tingly beef hand-ripped noodles, tiger vegetables salad*

JO: Sure it's fun to watch the skilled Chinese ladies roll, pull and rip noodles right before your eyes at X'ian Famous Foods (only at the Flushing location), but not as much as eating the noodles. When you order, ask for the degree of spiciness that suits your palate and be conservative. The sauce that's on these noodles is so delicious that diners actually discuss the best way to cook with the leftover drippings. And then there's the lamb burger. It's so deceptively simple. It's more like a pulled lamb sandiwch, aggressively spiced and exquisitely wrapped in the perfect bread. You have to taste it to understand its perfect beauty. A must eat.

manhattan

tribeca, financial district

eat

shop

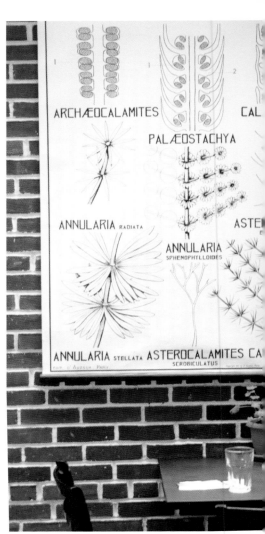

adeline
adeline

super friendly, stylish city bike shop

147 Reade Street
Between Greenwich and Hudson
(Tribeca) *map S57*
A/C/1/2/3: Chambers
212.227.1150
www.adelineadeline.com

twitter @adelinenyc
tues - sun noon - 6:30p
online shopping

Yes, Please: *linus dutchi bike (women), pashley guv'nor bike (men), retrovelo frame bag, yakkay helmet, crane copper bell, ortlieb bag, yepp kid's bike seat*

JO: I could not be happier to have a bike shop like Julie Hirschfeld's Adeline Adeline in my city. Recently I lived in a town where bikes were political and bike pros were not always friendly to novices like me. Bikes are too much fun to have shops that judge you for not embrocating before saddling up. Come to **Adeline Adeline** and you'll enjoy a completely different experience. You can test ride any of their gorgeous Dutch bikes plus buy a bevy of bells, helmets and baskets. When Julie whispers, "Why get all sweaty? You're biking to enjoy the ride to brunch, right?" you'll know you're in good hands.

barbarini

alimentari, mercato and ristorante

225 Front Street
Between Beekman and Peck Slip
(Financial District) *map E63*
2/3/4/5/J/Z/M: Fulton Street
A/C: Broadway - Nassau
212.227.8890
www.barbarinimercato.com

mon - fri 9:30a - 10:30p
sat - sun 11a - 9:30p
lunch. dinner. brunch. wine / beer. grocery
$$ reservations accepted

Yes, Please: *aranciata, espresso, speck, taleggio & frisee sandwich, ham & shredded eggs sandwich, grilled shrimp & avocado salad*

ERIGNOLA
.95/LB

CD: Italian men in leather coats will no doubt be sipping espresso outside of this very Italian mercato and alimentari. And inside **Barbarini**, you will find rows of pasta and canned tomatoes and a glass case bursting with sopressata and salami. Also gelati. Check. Olive oil and mostarda. Yes. Just about anything you can imagine in an Italian larder is sold here. You can also take a seat in the light-strewn back dining room and have the cooks make you something delicious like spaghetti with Sicilian tuna and capers. This place has authentic appeal, with the perfect touch of slickness on the finish.

blaue gans

a nyc wirtshaus

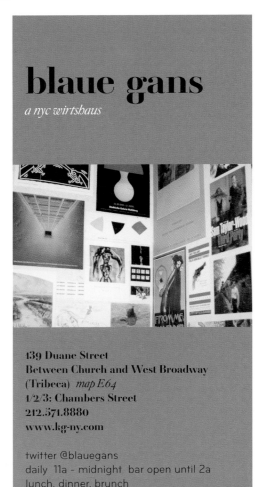

139 Duane Street
Between Church and West Broadway
(Tribeca) *map E64*
1/2/3: Chambers Street
212.571.8880
www.kg-ny.com

twitter @blauegans
daily 11a - midnight bar open until 2a
lunch. dinner. brunch
$$-$$$ reservations recommended

Yes. Please: *kônig pilsener, apfelschnaps, market bean salad with pistachios & sour cream, weibwurst & brezel, apple strudel with toasted almond ice cream*

KW: There are people who believe the only reason to eat is to fuel the body. Though I'm sure these folks have an enviously low body fat ratio, they are missing out on one of life's great pleasures: eating really good food. If you embrace self-deprivation, you might miss out on Kurt Gutenbrunner's mini-Austrian empire in NYC, which includes the fine dining mecca **Wallse**, **Café Sabarsky**, **The Upholstery Store**, and **Blaue Gans**, my favorite. This spot is a Bavarian-style gastropub where the neighborhood gathers to eat hearty, delicious fare. Health food it's not; happy food—absolutely.

nili lotan

downtown minimalism for women

188 Duane Street
Corner of Greenwich Street
(Tribeca) *map S58*
1/2/3: Chambers Street
212.219.8794
www.nililotan.com

twitter @nililotan
mon - sat noon - 7p sun noon - 6p

Yes, Please: *nili lotan: sloan dress, open stitch boyfriend sweater, cash shirt, spare cargo pant, cropped skinny jean, moleskin biker jacket*

KW: New York City is filled with all sorts of female urban breeds. There's the Upper East Siders with their sharp bobs, sharper heels and scarily perfect tailoring. Then there's the Brooklynites, who are often accompanied by their bearded mate and sometimes a cub. Then there are the Downtowners. They stay below 14th, wouldn't get caught with a spray tan and embrace fashion individuality. All three of these breeds could and would wear **Nili Lotan**. Her clothing is the essence of modern simplicity—classic and yet supremely urban. She's a best of her breed.

pasanella and son vintners

wine, spirits and drinking ephemera

115 South Street
Between Peck Slip and Beekman
(Financial District) *map S59*
A/C/2/3/4/5: Fulton Street /
Broadway - Nassau
212.233.8383
www.pasanellaandson.com

twitter @pasanellaandson
mon - sat 10a - 9p sun noon - 6p
onling shopping. classes

Yes, Please: *98 pol roger cuvee winston churchill,*
08 burlotto verduno pelaverga, pierre gimmonet brut nv,
black maple hill bourbon, marolo barolo grappa

CD: Despite the fact that I've spent the last decade as a food and wine writer, I often dreaded editing stories about the grape. I love wine, sure, and I know a fair share of oenophilic lingo—but, frankly, wine culture was just too serious for me. If, however, Marco Pasanella ruled the wine world, that would be another story. Shopping in his store **Pasanella and Son** makes wine and its accoutrements fun. From bottle stoppers in the shape of a horse's head to rare Barolos to a vintage car that acts as a wine display—shopping for a bottle here pleasantly erases all traces of my serious wine writer days.

philip williams posters

largest vintage poster gallery in the world

122 Chambers Street (entrance on Warren also)
Between Church and West Broadway (Tribeca) *map S60*
1/2/3: Chambers Street
212.513.0313
www.postermuseum.com

mon - sat 11a - 7p
online shopping. custom searches

Yes, Please: *posters: tourot muckens for philips, jacques barthes' nimes, furu's rosy rosy, niko's new mafia boss, razzias for harrods*

KW: My love of posters began in 1982 when I was in Spain during the World Cup. My brother and I snatched every one poster of the event that wasn't glued down. Later in the '80s I was studying in Japan and I was given an extraordinary poster by the designer Gan Hosoya. In the '90s I started collecting posters from Hatch Show Print in Nashville. Now it's a new century and I haven't bought any posters for a while. But that soon will be rectified at **Philip Williams**. I have no worries that I won't find something extraordinary here, because this place is vast with a capital V and the collection is awesome.

zibetto

italian espresso bar

102 Fulton Street
Corner of William
(Financial District) *map E65*
2/3/4/5/J/Z/M: Fulton Street
See website for other location
www.zibetto.com

mon - fri 7a - 7p sat 9a - 5p
sun 10a - 4p
coffee / tea. treats
$ cash only. first come, first served

Yes, Please: *cappuccino, hot chocolate, marocchino, affogato al caffe, aranciata, italian croissant, almond biscotti, caprese sandwich*

CD: As a West Coaster, I know that coffee culture dictates one must order a cup of coffee from a bearded barista, sit down with a laptop and remain seated for at least three hours. But nearly a decade spent living in NYC rendered me way too neurotic and high speed to ever embrace this lifestyle. Hence walking into **Zibetto** felt like coming home. The man behind the counter wore a crisp white button-up and a tie and was clean-shaven. And his cappuccinos and marocchinos? Inspired works of art. Customers stand at the counter while they imbibe, but they don't linger. They have better things to do.

finito

happy travels to you

rather *new york city*

isbn-13 9780984425358

every effort has been made to ensure the accuracy of the information in this book. however, certain details are subject to change. please remember when using the guides that hours alter seasonally and sometimes sadly, businesses close. the publisher cannot accept responsibility for any consequences arising from the use of this book.

editing / fact checking + production: chloe fields
in design master: nicole conant
map design + production: julia dickey + bryan wolf

thx to our friends at designers & agents for their hospitality and their support of the rather experience. please visit > designersandagents.com

rather is distributed by
independent publishers group > www.ipgbook.com

to peer further into the world of **rather** and to buy books, please visit **rather.com** to learn more